January 5, 2017

you came
with you
memories
times. Great joy and the
make of more memories

I hope I've touched your
Life in some way to help you.
to → **Come Closer**

to God

you have always been the
Sister I never had - I've
tried to keep up with where
you were and how you were.
hoping we could get back together and become close as

101 Days

we once
were

of Real Life Devotions

I love you my friend,
Sister-in-law, Sister in,
Christ pray we can some day
share Heaven together with
all our Loved-Ones and
friends. I pray you can
come for another visit soon

~~Dr. Doug LaPointe~~

January 12-2017

Love
Anna

P.S. try in some way
to lift <u>Jesus</u> daily

Come Close to God

ISBN: 978-1-5194-7159-8

To all those who are going through life
and who need to laugh,
to cry,
to feel,
to love,
and to come close
to God.

Acknowledgments

Cover design: Zgoda Design
Cover consultant: Lorie Fleenor
Editing: Triumph Communications, LLC
Typesetting: HemantLal@gmail.com
Editing: Cold Spring Men's Ministry
Proofing: Fran Presley
Production: Vinell Williams
Distribution: Cold Spring Church
Photography: Magic Moments Photography
Complicated graphs: None
Tables with lots of numbers: Not a one

Introduction

One day when I was speaking at a school, I spoke on the floor level and there was a stage behind me. A child was getting something up on that stage. His mother worked for the school and asked her son to fetch something up there even though my presentation was going on!

He was on the stage trying hard not to be noticed. Then, all of the sudden, he tripped and fell off the stage landing just to my left, a three foot drop. I looked over to see him face down on the ground. There was a full audience that saw the whole thing.

Now in that moment, that nanosecond when you think lots of things in a tiny space of time before you actually act or say something, I quickly went through all the files in my mind on what to do. You know, files on your response when someone falls off the stage behind you and lands at your feet in the middle of a message.

I quickly realized I had no file on that. Nothing. Empty. Who would have a file on that? No one. I quickly created my first file for it and said, "Are you okay?" He got up and brushed himself off without a word and left. I later found out he was fine alright, but his ego was a bit bruised for a while.

Moral of the story? You never know when you may end up in the center of attention with lots of eyes on you. Well, that's true of you right now. You actually are at the center of attention. Not of a group of people or in an embarrassing way, but from God Himself who loves you, died for you, and desires you to get closer to Him than you ever have been before.

The lights are on and the stage is set for you to come close to God! What will you do with this incredible challenge and opportunity from your great God? My hope and prayer is that you will use every moment of this opportunity – that all your energy will be given to it. The result is coming closer to God every day.

So, here is some help for the next 101 days. Let me join with you in your growth process, in this moment where God's eyes are upon you in His tremendous love.

"The eyes of the Lord are upon the righteous." (1 Peter 3:12)

Day 1

Night People, Morning People, and a Great Devotional Life

Daily is best!

One of the most important things for us to do every day is to have a great devotional life, time with God in His Word.

Ever notice how we can make time for lots of things, but find the devotional life is one of the first to get squeezed out? Knowing how important it is, Paul said, "Let the word of Christ dwell in you richly."

You join with the great saints of all time when you keep a good devotional life. Joshua said he meditates on God's Word day and night. David rose early to praise Him.

Someone once said that a devotional life is like food. You can miss a meal but eventually you will suffer. Yes, you can miss a day here or there of devotions, but it needs to be a very regular habit.

Things you do on a daily basis have a great power in your life – time with kids, brushing your teeth, and yes, eating to name a few. What would life be like if we skipped these important daily things? Over time, not good.

The same is true of our spiritual life when we miss a lot of our daily devotions.

What great power when your daily life features time with God.

Internalize this:

> **Do not let this Book of the Law depart from your mouth; meditate on it day and night, so that you may be careful to do everything written in it. Then you will be prosperous and successful.**
>
> **Joshua 1:8**

How is that fair?!

I've noticed that the world seems to favor morning people. Let me give you a few examples. If you send someone an e-mail at say, 7:00 am, you will be highly regarded for being industrious, getting up early to start the day. Now, send someone an e-mail at say, 1:00 am, and they will think you're strange. "Why didn't you just go to bed?" they will ask. Same e-mail, same content. No matter, you are strange to them.

Do a lot of work before breakfast and you'll be regarded as having a great work ethic. People say things like, "I plowed a field and walked five miles to deliver chickens – all before breakfast." It sounds so good. Do a lot of work after midnight and people will wonder why you bothered to stay up. Same work, same amount. They say, "I plowed a field and walked five miles to deliver chickens – all after midnight." It sounds so bad.

Eat a good breakfast and people say you're wise to start your day that way. Eat a big meal at midnight, and you're likely to have weight problems. Same food!

My night person and morning person fight each other. I stay up late watching a great show. I wake up and my morning person says, "What have you done? You have a big day today. You can't be all tired." The morning person is always the reasonable one and always wins the argument.

I seriously believe had school started at say, 8:00 pm, and ended at say, 2:00 am, I would've gotten straight A's. Instead, we were at the bus stop near dawn. I'm surprised I passed.

There is a rhythm to your day – times that work better for you than other times. Maybe you're a morning person, maybe not. These times may change over the years. A good goal is to figure out where in your day a devotional works best. For some it's in the morning, some it is the evening, some after lunch or some other time. Then you are far more likely to make it a habit. You are more likely to let His Word dwell in you richly.

Let a good devotional life powerfully change you and, over time, do marvelous things in your life.

Know that things done daily always do.

Reading: Colossians 3:1-17

"Things you do daily have great power in your life."

Day 2

A Golf Instructor's Most Feared Question and Patience in the Process of Growth

Why is it taking so long!?

Everyone jokes about standing in front of the microwave, arms crossed, tapping your foot in impatience, and while it's kind of a funny visual, it's not far off.

It's a fact: in your life, you're called to (and capable of) accomplishing great things in the Lord and of growing a close and deep relationship with Him.

The thing is it doesn't happen right away. It takes time, effort, and hard work to get there. Even with intense desire and commitment, it still takes time and hard work. Sit back and wait for it to happen, and you'll never get there. Give up on the process and you'll never get there that way either.

Growth is a matter of striving, fighting, pulling, pushing, keeping going… and keeping going some more. We are to "press on" and "strain forward".

No wonder the Bible urges us to the hard work of growth telling us to be like an "enduring soldier", "disciplined athlete", and "hardworking farmer".

No wonder we call patience a virtue and must look down the road a bit, not live only for immediate results. Proverbs says, "Where there is no vision, the people perish."

It's all needed for growth.

Internalize this:

> **Forgetting what is behind and straining toward what is ahead, I press on toward the goal to win the prize for which God has called me heavenward in Christ Jesus.**
>
> **Philippians 3:13-14**

Nobody got hurt… at least not seriously.

For many years, I taught golf to classes for the Parks Department. Unfortunately for me, I taught golfers in the worst phase of any golfer's career – the start. I can't even count the number of bad shots I've seen (and ducked).

Sometimes I yearned to be one of those instructors who is refining someone's game that was great already. I could be like, "Everything's perfect now just move that left pinky over a tad. You will hit it 320 yards instead of the 310 you've been getting."

No. I didn't teach any golfer in that phase.

The shots of my students were more likely to kill squirrels than to leave the ground. They were little grounders that went 30 yards or so. Some were only say, three yards away. Some, three feet. Some didn't move at all.

It was after those shots that I would often hear my most dreaded question. With the ball still right next to them, they look up and ask, "How was that?"

"How was what?" I'm thinking. "Oh, you mean that shot you just took? You do know the ball is right there, right?" But I gave a better reply, "You know this takes time, hard work, and perseverance. Apply those things and you'll get there."

Now some of those golfers went on to become good golfers. In fact, all the great golfers you see started out pretty much like that… a trickly little shot followed by the dreaded question, "How's that?"

Remember the hard work that most everything takes. Do the work that spiritual growth takes – the striving, fighting, pulling, pushing, and keeping going.

Never compromise. Always keep learning and persevering. Be sure to be patient too and realize the process you are in. Press on! Strain forward!

Just like golfers who have become great, know you will get great results in your walk with God.

Reading: Philippians 3:7-14 and 4:4-9

"Just about everything you do now once seemed impossible to you."

Day 3

Most Likely To Go Bald
and Who God Uses

"I can't do it."

Ever evaluated yourself when it comes to thinking about how much God will work in and through you... and think you come up short?

Maybe you figured you will not be used that much... just not skilled enough, just not the greatest talent.

But, no, God is not choosing based on our skills or perceived lack of them. He always uses us if we're *willing* – no matter what we've got going for us or against us by way of "talent".

This desire to be used is actually the key. That is, really wanting to be used by God and willing to let it happen – saying to God, "Send me."

Coming to the conclusion that He will or won't use you based on your "talent" is absurd to Him – even bordering on offensive. It's His skill that matters, not yours, and He's got plenty of it.

Scripture even says that God chooses the foolish things of the world to shame the wise and the weak things of the world to shame the strong.

Surely He will use you and me.

Internalize this:

> **Then I heard the voice of the Lord saying,**
> **'Whom shall I send? And who will go for us?'**
> **And I said, 'Here am I. Send me!'**

> **Isaiah 6:8**

"Most Popular, "Best Athlete", "Most Likely to Succeed"

Like everyone, when I was in high school I wanted to receive one of those yearbook superlative awards. Mind you, I wasn't picky. Any one of those awards would have been great by me.

Well, I didn't actually win any. But fortunately for me, I had a second chance when I became a school teacher. They voted on superlatives every year and teachers were included.

I thought, "Alright, I'm sure to win sooner or later. I'll just never retire if I have to." Well, sure enough, I eventually did win. The category of my victory, however, was not one of those great ones I had in mind when I hoped to win. No, it wasn't like those at all. I won in a category I didn't even know existed:

"Most Likely to Go Bald"

And I had to share it with another guy. And he was pretty much already bald. I asked the students, "What do you mean by bald? Like, a little hair loss or something?" "No." They said. "We mean bald. Bald, bald. Cue ball bald. That's right, you're the winner. We believe in YOU for that."

Like "Best Teacher" instead would've killed them.

I protested at first and the Principal didn't like when she found out about this category either. But I told her with a certain amount of defeat in my voice, "Hey, let it go. At least I won. Well, co-won."

How silly though when we take stock of our talents and think we will be used if we have a lot. How silly to think we will not be used if we think we have little. No way. Instead seek to be available to God and you will be used.

Be ready to be used greatly of God whether you were voted "Most Likely to Succeed" or "Most Likely to Go Bald".

Or nothing at all.

Reading: 1 Corinthians 1:18-2:5

**"God does not choose the able,
He enables those He chooses."**

Day 4

A Half-Dead Flower
and How God Sees You

More than six billion people on the planet. Nearly seven, actually.

And rising! So some feel, "How on earth could I possibly matter much?" "After all, God's got His hands full, right? And if He's kind of busy, why should I believe I matter all that much?"

This sure is how lots and lots of people feel – that life's just passing by, day in and day out without God or any person taking notice of them. They feel inconsequential, insignificant, unnoticed, part of the crowd.

But Jesus' cross says something entirely different. In the cross, you were counted absolutely worthy, valuable enough for God to die for you.

You may have heard that even if you were the only person on earth, Jesus would have gone through all that He did just for you.

It's also true that while He was dying on the cross, He was thinking of you.

Someone once said if God had a refrigerator, it would be your picture on it. If He were writing a modern history book, He wouldn't just include the things everyone regards as big. He would write about you.

What amazing love and care God has just for you.

Internalize this:

> **For God so loved the world that he gave his one and only Son, that whoever believes in him shall not perish but have eternal life.**

> **John 3:16**

This woman was a saint… and a bus driver!

I can't remember her name, but she drove my school bus day after day – filled with screaming, jumping, bouncing, laughing little kids. It wasn't like she talked to me in particular, or gave out candy, or anything else memorable – she was just a nice lady.

So one day, I wanted to do something nice for her.

I picked a flower from my neighbor's yard (please, don't tell anyone), wrapped it with a wet paper towel, and put it next to my backpack to give to my bus driver. The next day I got on and handed it to her.

Now, when you're a kid, there are thousands of things going on every day. And most of them are quickly and permanently forgotten.

But, her reaction to my little (and half-dead) gift stuck with me.

The expression on her face said, "I had no idea that anyone was noticing me at all. It matters so much that you do."

You may not realize just how much God's noticing you and counting you as so loved and so important.

But, He is.

Know He so loved you, He sent His Son to die for you.

Realize that God is always directing His 100% attention toward you with great care – no matter how many people there are.

In the midst of the hustle and bustle, know He is giving flowers to you all the time. He always notices and always appreciates you.

Live in the great assurance of your infinite significance to God.

Receive those flowers.

Reading: 1 John 4:7-11

"How God sees you means everything."

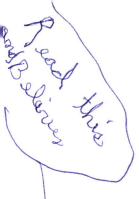

Day 5

Surviving Alligators
and Surviving Death

You're going to die.

Well not now hopefully, but someday. As a result of our sin, it's inevitable. No one escapes physical death. But, here's the good news. Christ has defeated the curse of sin and death by His death on the cross.

Sin and death are beaten. The victory is in Christ. We can be forgiven in Him and live forever. His resurrection demonstrated His victory over death. He rose from the dead to live forevermore. We will be united with Him in his resurrection if we have welcomed Him into our life! We will rise too!

That's the whole point of why He came, and you can know with certainty that He's preparing a place for you to live forever (a glorious, joyful, radiant, abundant, purpose-filled, and wholly lovely forever) with Him.

The Bible says, "Our Savior, Christ Jesus... has destroyed death and has brought life and immortality to light through the gospel." We all die physically, but we can all live on forever with God through Christ, in glory.

And, the most important thing is that we are forgiven and have eternal life.

Internalize this:

**I am the resurrection and the life.
He who believes in me will live even if he dies;
and whoever lives and believes in me will never die.**

John 11:25-26

Ever seen those *Worst Case Scenario Survival* books?

They give you step-by-step instructions on how to survive just about anything. One dilemma it talks about is how to survive an attack by an alligator. I'm not too sure it will work. My comments are in the parentheses.

1) If you are on land, try to get on the alligator's back. *(No, I don't think so.)*
2) Cover the alligator's eyes. *(I'd rather cover my own eyes.)*
3) Use any weapon you have. *(I would have put that first.)*
4) If its jaws close on something you want to remove such as a limb, punch it on the snout. *(I guess with one of the limbs you have left.)*
5) If the alligator gets you in its jaws, you must prevent it from shaking you. This will cause severe tissue damage. *(No kidding!)*
6) Seek medical attention immediately. *(I like this vote of confidence here at the end. And notice it says "immediately" like it wouldn't be first on my 'to do' list with all that tissue damage.)*

It goes on to say that we must not try to "capture" it. *(Not a problem.)*

Then it adds that in Florida, alligators can be in any water but then says, "Do not swim or wade alone, and always check the area before venturing in." *(You just said there can be alligators in there and now you're telling me to… venture in?! And to bring a friend?!)*

These books can tell you how to survive a lot of things though. But they can't tell you how to survive death and live forever. And really, if you think about it, death is the most important thing to survive. It's our greatest need.

For that, we need the Bible. Know it has clearly told us that death is defeated in Christ. Know He has paid the penalty of our sin. Surviving death is completely open to us in Him. Know that in Christ, you will never die.

If you've never accepted Christ into your life and heart, why not invite Him in using this prayer? If you have already, rejoice that you will escape death and live forever.

"Jesus, I am sorry that I have kept you out of my life. Thank you for dying on the cross for my sins. I open the door of my heart and receive you now. Come into my life. I want to be forgiven and restored to you and begin the relationship with you I was always meant to have. Thank you for receiving all who come to you and giving forgiveness and eternal life."

Reading: 1 Cor. 15:51-58 and 2 Timothy 1:8-10

"The most important thing to survive is death."

Day 6

The Friendly Skies
and Really Loving Others from the Heart

"Love one another as I have loved you." Sounds simple enough. But what's it really mean? How do you know whether you're really doing it?

Real love – the way God calls us to love – looks a bit like this: The outcome of other's lives really matters to you. You passionately desire the best for others – even if it means personal sacrifice. In fact, it's been said that the opposite of love is not hatred but indifference.

So, when we love, the needs of others are really our concern. It's not so much a mooshy feeling. It's a commitment of service to others really seeing God loves them and responding to that.

It's not just to people we know and like. It's to strangers too and people who actually have personally done us harm. It extends to our friends and enemies. It's not done for what we may get back but to those who could never repay us. This is the kind of love God has for you – made obvious by His sacrifice on the cross for you.

So we read, "While we were yet sinners, Christ died for us."

Internalize this:

> **Love is patient, love is kind. It does not envy, it does not boast, it is not proud. It is not rude, it is not self-seeking, it is not easily angered, it keeps no record of wrongs.**

> **1 Corinthians 13:4-5**

Hot coffee, coming through!

I was about to board a flight thinking my seat was in Row 3. Great! I figured the best plan was to wait for everyone else to get on the plane and then just walk on and take my seat… in Row 3. And what could be nicer than getting a cup of hot coffee to take on-board?

Piping hot coffee in hand, I started to board, double checking my seat assignment only to find it's not Row 3! It's Row 23. Okay, now that's not good. I had my bags, my hot coffee, and… my two-year old son!

I did not count on those extra 20 rows which now seemed about a mile down that tiny aisle. Now I stood at the front of the plane with my bags hanging way off to the right and left of my body. I was too wide to get down the row and my arms were full.

Then she stood up. This lady in about the sixth row, and she said, "Can I hold your coffee?" "Yes!" Handing her my coffee, I thought, now I had a chance.

I started heading down the aisle. I could feel my bags smacking and smashing into everyone on both sides as I went. Now, we're not talking about the bags just brushing people. These were real hits. Yet they didn't even seem to mind.

In fact, as I went a little further, I noticed all the people were even smiling at me. (Of course I later figured it out that they were actually smiling at my two-year old. But, it felt good.)

Finally made it to my seat, and as soon as I sat down, the lady who had taken my coffee delivered it to me – with a smile! As I sat, I thought to myself, "These people were rooting for me! They cared how this whole thing ended up. They sacrificed for me."

And, if we wonder if we're loving others, we can just ask: Do we take the initiative in people's lives like that lady with my coffee? Are we patient when their life's baggage hits us like when mine hit them? Do we look for the best in people as they come our way just as my fellow passengers did that day? Do we go the extra mile like that delivery?

You know, because of all that, the aisle of that plane on that day seemed really wide to me. By what you do and say, you make the aisle of other people's lives wider or more narrow. Let the life of others really matter to you… love them.

Make the aisle wider.

Reading: 1 John 4:15-5:3

"By what we do and say, we can make the aisle of others' lives much wider or more narrow."

Day 7

100 Yellow Ribbons
and Coming Back to God

God: "Nope. Sorry. You've messed up too much."
You or me: "Yeah, I thought so. Sorry for bothering you."

For many, that's the way the conversation in their heads goes with God. They think they're just too bad or let God down just too many times for Him to take them back and love them.

Is the conversation like that for you? At least on some level, are you unsure of how God really feels about you so that you can't really believe He'd want you and forgive you? "Oh, you have no idea what I have done. God would never accept me." Or, "I have left Him so many times, He won't take me back now," your heart says.

Not so. Receiving those who have strayed is the whole point of why Christ died and rose again. No sin is too great that it is not covered by the cross.

Grace. Mercy. That's what God's all about offering to anyone willing to return to Him and receive. In fact, God rejoices more over one who returns than 99 who are already His. And if you ever stray, He receives you yet again with great joy.

This is our wonderful God. This is the great mercy and love shown to us in Jesus.

This is His love that never fails.

Internalize this:

> **If we confess our sins, he is faithful and just and will forgive us our sins and purify us from all unrighteousness.**
>
> **1 John 1:9**

"Please let it be there!"

When I was a kid, there was a big hit song called "Tie a Yellow Ribbon 'Round the Old Oak Tree". It was by Tony Orlando and Dawn and was based on a true story. Many of you remember it well.

The song was about a man who went to prison. He had been there three years but was now about to get out. He had a girlfriend before he went to jail. Now, three years later, he hoped she still wanted him but wasn't sure.

So, he wrote her a letter to tell her he was coming out. He wrote in effect, "If you still want me, this is what I want you to do. The bus that will be taking me out of jail will come to my house where there is the old oak tree in the front."

"If you still want me, tie a yellow ribbon 'round the old oak tree. If I see it there, I'll know you still want me. If not, I'll stay on the bus, forget about us, and put the blame on me."

As the song goes, when the bus approached the tree the man couldn't bear to look. He wanted so much to see a yellow ribbon there and he wasn't at all sure whether he would. The others on the bus knew what was going on. They were looking out the window for him – kinda wondering about the whole outcome too.

Suddenly, the guy hears the whole bus cheering so he looks out. There were 100 yellow ribbons 'round the old oak tree. She wanted him back that much.

And, there are 100 yellow ribbons 'round the old oak tree from God to you… no matter what you've done. And all you have to do is turn back around and let Him love you.

If you've strayed, come back. If you have never come to the Lord, receive Him! Accept His unconditional love.

Respond to those 100 yellow ribbons from God.

They're up!

Reading: Luke 15:1-24

"God's forgiveness always comes, not because our sin isn't so bad, but because His grace is so good."

Day 8

Accepting New Inventions
and Accepting New Things from God

Reluctant to change?

The fact is, we can all have a resistance to change which may be keeping us from the things God desires. We just won't let them happen.

Change means risk, challenge, and discomfort – things many people are not willing to take on. It happens on an individual basis and in groups, too. Many churches are the least willing to do a new thing.

It's not that all change is good but that a lot of it is. And, changing things just for the sake of change isn't the point either. But certain change we must have. We would be missing out on so much.

Often we don't even know we are having resistance to change. It just comes out in sentiments like, "That will never work." "I don't need that." "Things are good enough the way they are."

The Bible tells us that God constantly desires to do great things, new things in our lives. It's part of what the Bible means when it tells us to "sing a new song" to God. We are to sing a new song because He has done a new thing. Being more open to the right kind of change may usher in many new things from God.

Just like He wants it.

Internalize this:

> **Sing to the Lord a new song; sing to the Lord, all the earth.**
> **Sing to the Lord, praise his name; proclaim his salvation.**

> **Psalm 96:1-2**

I'm the pot calling the kettle black here.

Resistance to change has shown up in my life in how I've responded to technology when each new thing first comes out. Here's how I've responded to a few inventions during my life. Maybe it's the same for you?

TV remote: "How lazy, we can't just get up?"

Answering machine: "Just call back. I'll be home."

CDs: "What's wrong with records and cassettes… and 8-tracks?"

Personal computer: "Now what would I need that for?"

GPS: "I can just ask someone if I get lost."

Cell Phone: "That's why I have an answering machine!"

I'm afraid to think what my reaction would have been to some of the greatest inventions of all time had I been there… Electric light bulb: "Like the sun isn't enough!" Flight: "Great, now my in-laws will always be over." Automobile: "But, I love my horse!" And I did this with all those sentiments like "That will never work." "I don't need that." "Things are good enough the way they are."

And, I'm not alone. Look what some others have said:

"This 'telephone' has too many shortcomings to be seriously considered as a means of communication." Western Union internal memo, 1876.

"Heavier-than-air flying machines are impossible." Lord Kelvin, physicist, 1895.

"There is no reason anyone would want a computer in their home." Ken Olson, Founder of Digital Equipment Corp., 1977.

"Everything that can be invented has been invented." Charles H. Duell, Commissioner, U.S. Office of Patents, 1899.

Yet, just like these inventions, God has new and great things planned for your life. Ask Him to show you what change is good and from Him.

Be aware of your own reluctance and resistance to change. Be open to new things from God. Be willing to be challenged, to take on what He has for you. Embrace discomfort and risk to do so. Be aware of all you can miss out on through your resistance. Be certain you experience all the new and wonderful things God desires to do in your life.

Sing to Him a new song.

Reading: Exodus 15:1-21

"Resistance to change may mean resistance to great things from God."

Day 9

50 Sextillion-to-one Odds and the God of the Impossible

Some situations can be very tough in life.

Maybe we've been laid off, have a tough relationship with our teen, been diagnosed with a serious illness. In the natural, from our perspective, there are many things that can seem downright impossible. In the natural, maybe they are!

But, not so with God. God can do the impossible. He doesn't have the limitations we may unconsciously think He does. He is much greater than we will ever know. He raises the dead and calls into being what does not exist – the "impossible".

So, when all is said and done, we have no need to wonder if God can do what He desires in our life. He can. A tough marriage, rough finances, an unsaved loved one? We can have complete trust in the one who can do anything.

If God wants it done, it's done.

How great is our God!

Internalize this:

I can do everything through him who gives me strength.

Philippians 4:13

1,000,000,000,000,000,000,000

Sports columnists are always trying to calculate the odds of each team in a particular sport winning it all that year. So a team might be listed at say 10 to 1 to win the World Series or 16 to 1 to win the Super Bowl.

It struck me when the NCAA college basketball playoffs were beginning one year and they showed the odds of all 64 teams in the tournament.

The team with the best odds was 3 to 1. These are good odds, a 1 in 3 chance of winning it all with 64 teams involved. But, I glanced down to the team with the worst odds to win at the start of the tournament and it was Jackson State of Mississippi. They gave Jackson State these odds: 50 Sextillion to 1.

What?! Was I reading that right? Did they really think that school only had a 50 sextillion to 1 chance of winning? I didn't even know that sextillion was a number. Did you?

Whatever that number is, I thought, it must be really big and if that number is really big, Jackson State's odds of winning are ridiculously small. (The number is just below the memory verse.)

I mean, the odds of getting struck by lightning are only like a million to 1. You'd have a better chance of getting struck by lightning several times before Jackson State would win this tournament. Other teams fared only a little better. One was at 25 Sextillion to 1. They were twice as likely to win as Jackson State. One was at a billion to 1, a veritable shoo-in compared to Jackson State.

If I were the coach of any of these teams I would have said to them, "Whatever you do, don't read the paper today."

Well, Jackson State didn't win that year. True enough. But one of the things to be very careful of in life is to think that something God wants done can't be done. Even if the odds, naturally speaking were 50 sextillion to 1, if God chooses it to be done, it's done.

Know He will accomplish the things in life He desires to... no matter the odds. Know He can do anything in your life He wants done... no matter how hard they may seem.

Trust and believe.

And stand in awe of the greatness of our God.

Reading: Judges 7:1-25

"If God wants it done, the odds of it are 1 to 1."

Day 10

The Jefferson Edited Bible
and the Authority of God's Word

Can God misspeak?

Some believers seem to think so. By believing only certain parts of the Bible, for whatever reason, they limit their own effectiveness in life and in their relationship with God.

The Bible is truly the word of God. Accurate in every detail.

In its pages we find God's message to us. Just as God cannot err neither is even one word in His Word in error.

The Bible shows us clearly the way to start a relationship with God, be right with God, and get to heaven. It covers our greatest needs, to know Him and be forgiven. And it can be completely relied upon as accurate.

The Bible is like a love letter from God showing us exactly how to relate with Him and how to grow closer to Him.

It covers, at least in principle, everything. It gives us perfect guidance for any issue we'll ever face in life and for any decision we'll ever need to make.

True power comes into your life when you really embrace the Bible with your whole heart and know it's all true.

God can't err.

Internalize this:

> **All Scripture is God-breathed and is useful for teaching, rebuking, correcting and training in righteousness so that the servant of God may be thoroughly equipped for every good work.**
>
> **2 Timothy 3:16-17**

A great president. A lousy editor. Thomas Jefferson, a founding father of this nation, and a genius when it came to government. As Americans, we're all indebted to him. This is true.

However, did you know that Thomas Jefferson made his own 'translation' of the Bible?

He went through the Bible, picking out the things he didn't believe and leaving in the things he liked. In the end, he took out all the miracles and supernatural events because he refused to believe these things.

He even took out the resurrection of Jesus, showing His victory over sin and death. He left out the essential message of Jesus Christ rising from the dead.

You guessed it. In the end, Jefferson ended up with a much smaller version of the Bible when what was left were the only parts he believed. It is called The Jefferson Bible. It actually still exists.

Many of us do the very same thing with the Word of God. (But without the scissors.) We pick the parts we want to believe and reject the rest. It's like taking a love letter from your wife and cutting out all the parts you don't believe in until it looks like one of those cutout snowflakes kids make.

Imagine saying, "Honey, look what I did to your note. I cut out all the parts I did not agree with." (Men, do not try this!) Or, it's like taking parts out of a perfectly working engine. It won't work that way – and forget about adding extra parts in instead. That just makes for a different kind of disaster.

You might not go as far as Jefferson in making your own version, but when you take out parts you don't believe, accepting contrary teaching instead, it's the same end result.

The Bible is all correct. Let this be the conviction of your heart. Let the authority of God's Word be the basis of your life.

Know it's God-breathed.

Reading: Psalm 119:97-105

"Just as God can't make a mistake, so His Word is without error."

Day 11

A Zebra in the Woods
and Letting God Surprise Us

It's almost a cliché by now but it is certainly true that God's ways are not our ways. He does things we don't expect, we didn't see coming.

It's important to know this and appreciate this since it keeps us from having to see things happen only in the ways we expect. It keeps us from putting God in a box (uh-oh, another cliché) and has us ready for everything He might choose to do and how He might choose to do it.

Accepting God's higher ways also helps us to have hope in the mighty things to come. After all, He can accomplish His ways in just about any manner. How exciting!

So, Paul says God's ways are "unsearchable… and His paths beyond tracing out."

Ever notice how many of the great things that have happened to you came when or in a way you didn't expect? History is the same. Who could have seen the slaying of Goliath come the way it did? Who would have seen the Red Sea parting before it happened?

Needing things to happen a certain way may prevent them.

God will surprise us.

Internalize this:

> **As the heavens are higher than the earth,**
> **so are my way higher than your ways**
> **and my thoughts than your thoughts.**

> **Isaiah 55:9**

Let me out!

To this day, I'm not sure why, but the park I served as golf instructor sent me on a park tour. I was to be shown all the area parks of the county just to see them. I'm sure you can feel the excitement I had over this idea coming off the page right now.

Well sure enough, it began very uneventfully. Then, as we were riding in one of the parks, suddenly, in the distance, I saw a zebra. Now this was definitely a zebra. You know when you see a zebra or not. That's why they have stripes… so you'll know. You don't ask "Is that a horse?" No. It has stripes. This one had stripes. It was a zebra… and this was in a park, in the woods of New Jersey.

Last I checked, the population of zebras in NJ was not high.

Oddly though, the Park Ranger leading our tour didn't even mention it. You would think that if you are on a boring park tour in New Jersey and a zebra enters the scene, you would at least point that kind of thing out. Nope. Not a word.

Well, as we got a little closer, I could see that there was a chain-link fence between us and the zebra, deep in the woods. We had come up next to a safari that was just on the other side of the park.

Voila, a zebra.

Gee, would the Park Ranger have said anything if we came up against the rhino or tiger section or would he just have let me sweat that out?

A lot of what God does will be just like seeing that zebra. It is out in left field to us. It is a surprise. He will do things we do not expect all the time.

Learn to expect the unexpected, higher ways of God. Keep alert to things you may otherwise miss. Let things happen God's unexpected way.

Be hopeful and open to what God chooses to do.

Be open to "zebras".

Reading: Isaiah 55:1-13

"Zebras happen."

Day 12

Native Americans Helping Colonists and Fighting the Good Fight

We are called to fight the good fight.

But, so often with Christians the weapons of our warfare are obvious but we don't even use them. We've got great resources at our disposal to help us win every battle in the Lord.

We have shields, helmets, swords, and everything else. They are: the power of the Holy Spirit, prayer, knowing and following the Bible, fellowship, being in ministry, active church life, and so much more.

We become prepared for battle with them, walking in the truth, abiding in faith. We become strong and mighty in Christ.

David once said, "It is God who arms me with strength… He trains my hands for battle… you give me your shield of victory."

But instead we often go by our own strength. We pray only occasionally. We read the Bible every so often. We stay disconnected from other believers. We don't fully engage in meaningful ministry. We miss church far too often. Our armor's on the ground.

Some then waffle in and out of truth, faith, trust, and all that pleases God. We are exposed to defeat, fighting unprepared, losing battles.

Instead, we are called to win them.

Internalize this:

> **The weapons we fight with are not the weapons of the world. On the contrary, they have divine power to demolish strongholds.**

2 Corinthians 10:4

History tells us that the American Colonists were pretty much getting whipped by the British, but the story doesn't end that way. Just in time, the Native Americans taught some of the Colonists how to fight.

Standing in lines in open fields, wearing bright colored uniforms, yelling, "Ready! Aim! Fire!" That's how the Red Coats of Britain fought – and the Colonists copied their style. As one line of soldiers fell, the next line moved up. It was very ineffective.

Then the Native Americans, who knew how to fight using the element of surprise and all, trained these Colonists. I would have loved to have been there for this conversation.

The Native Americans are like, "Hey, I don't mean to interrupt. I know you are busy with your war here and everything. But, you know, when you fight you ought to maybe consider, like, getting behind a tree or something. That way, when the bullets come your way, they hit the tree. That really is much better than hitting you, ya' know?"

"And, don't wear bright colored clothing that stands out like the British do. I mean, don't get me wrong. You look good in blue and all. But, you might want to try something that blends with what's behind you. Something that looks like trees and dirt would be good. Because again, if they miss and hit the tree, that's a good thing. Living really should be your goal here."

"Oh… one more thing. Don't announce when you're gonna fire. Just do it. This 'Ready! Aim! Fire!' thing you're doing is not really the way to go. Just shoot. Shoot the gun!"

So, where in your life do you find yourself standing in an open field, wearing bright colors, and yelling "Fire!" by not using your weapons?

Fight wisely! Read the Bible. Pray. Fellowship in a good church. Be in ministry. Walk by the Holy Spirit.

Pick up your armor!

Demolish strongholds… and see victory.

Reading: 2 Samuel 22:1-7, 26-40

"Fighting unprepared is no way to fight."

Day 13

Twenty-Seven Year Olds in Youth Group and Giving Up on No One

Ever been tempted to give up on someone? You know, think they'll never come to the Lord?

Maybe they just never show an interest in God and salvation so we figure they never will. Some marriages are like this. One spouse hopes and prays for years for the other one to come to the Lord. Or maybe it's your kids, who, as they grew up, showed no interest in following God.

It can be really easy to despair and think there's no hope for that person – that nothing will ever change. But the Bible tells us to be filled with hope at all times for every person, that God is full of hope for every person. Even when you're about to give up on someone, God's not even close to giving up.

God is patient with everyone, not desiring any to perish but all to come to the saving knowledge of Christ. He constantly seeks to find them drawing them to Himself.

At any moment, that person you love – who's never even given the slightest indication they're even close – can come to Christ.

Many do!

Internalize this:

> **The promise is for you and your children and for all who are far off – for all whom the Lord our God will call.**

> **Acts 2:39**

It was a youth group night, and I'll never forget when these two 'kids' showed up. Now I say 'kids' but they looked like they were 26 or 27. I'm not sure. Perhaps they failed a grade, or nine grades.

Didn't take me long to realize they weren't at youth group for the normal reasons. Turns out they had come to fulfill community service obligations they had because of trouble with the law.

I guess the judge decreed they could either do jail time or be with me. At least they chose me.

I don't know what they did to get arrested, but based on the amount of community service they had, it must've been real bad. I tried to keep my eye on them but it was particularly difficult since they were identical twins. It felt like they were all over.

They lurked on the fringes of the event and seemed as uninterested as humanly possible. I think they snuck out for a smoke from time to time. I figured they would come a few times to youth group and that would be it.

Well, that was it, they did stop coming – for a while anyway. Then one of them not only came back but had graduated from high school and wanted to help lead with us. He said that he had accepted Christ and everything had changed for him.

He helped out for several months, and it was clear he really had accepted Christ. He continued to help faithfully. Then one day, we asked him to speak to the youth group at a fireside talk we were having during a camp outing. He told the group, "You would never have thought that I would have gone from where I was to where I am now."

He was right. That is exactly what I was thinking. Then he said, "Never give up on anyone." He went off to college to influence his campus for the Lord too.

Know this happens all the time. Never give up on the people in your life. Keep praying. Keep showing them how to walk with God with your own life.

Know God hasn't given up on them either and is working on them even today!

Believe the promise is for those who are "far off" too.

Reading: Acts 9:1-18

"The most lost often turn around the most dramatically."

Day 14

Removing Pet-stained Carpet and Removing Pet Sins

Not all pets are nice.

Our life can greatly be determined by a pet sin or two we keep with us. You know, the things you may do and decide you're just going to let slide in your life.

A pet sin usually doesn't stay confined to one part of your life though. It can't be caged. Pet sins escape touching everything else and leaving you wondering how one pet sin has affected you so much!

There is an expression and it goes like this "If Jesus is not Lord of all, He is not Lord at all." It sort of says all pet sins must go.

Now, it's not so much a sense of perfection that's demanded. We will not hit that. But it is a call to not settle in our life with behaviors that shouldn't be there.

What it means is that our highest priority is God. It means we recognize the effect any sin will have on the rest of our life and seek its removal. It means we realize that if we continue, the pet sin and its effects get bigger over time.

Every pet you feed grows.

Pet sins should be left to starve.

Internalize this:

> **I am the Lord your God; consecrate yourselves and be holy, because I am holy.**
>
> **Leviticus 11:44**

These neighbors are strict!

One time when my family moved, it was particularly tough. We had just gotten in the house and removed the old carpet and put it outside in the back. That carpet really had to go. It was smelly and badly stained.

The next day, in the mailbox was a notice telling us to get the debris out of our yard! I couldn't believe it! We just moved in! We just put that carpet out there! I didn't even know anyone could see it! We have a fenced backyard!

This neighborhood is vigilante about yard debris! What happened to those days when the first notice you get is a welcome to the neighborhood? And you get that notice in person complete with pie!? Where was my pie?

Now it had rained on the carpet. Carpet is heavy. Wet carpet is almost immovable at least for one person… that's all I had… after all, I was new… I hadn't met the neighbors to ask for help.

I hadn't gotten any pie.

How 'bout a bonfire? I could burn the carpet and grab some marshmallows, invite all the neighbors and tell them it was a welcoming party. Someone would be there and be like "Do I smell… carpet?" Plus, I'd probably be breaking another community ordinance for fire…. they probably have some ordinance for marshmallows too! (Yes, I was getting a bit sour about my new neighborhood.)

There was no other way that wet carpet was getting out of there, though. Well, to my relief, I found out that the notice about yard debris was simply left in the mailbox for the previous owners. The notice had nothing to do with my carpet.

But, a pet sin, though, is like that wet, smelly, ugly carpet in your backyard. It's so bad and gets harder and harder to remove. And, the longer it's there, the worse it gets.

Keep pet sins out now before they get so hard to remove. Remove any you may have let in. Let pet sins starve. Make Christ Lord of all.

Be holy for He is holy.

Reading: Matthew 5:17-48

"Leave pet sins to starve."

Day 15

The Right Answers about Whiskers and the Right Answers about Life

"Doesn't matter if you climb the ladder of success, if your ladder's up against the wrong tree."

That's for sure. Without the right goal, "success" is basically like winning at losing. When our goals and aim are off, it's like life has us by the tail. We are just getting tossed around. You've got to know what you need to be doing and being in life in order to succeed.

The most important of these things is to follow God with all your heart. This decision gives you the right priorities and focus that makes your life all it should be.

Cain was called a "restless wanderer" on the earth. It describes everyone without the right aim in life.

We're told just how to be on the right path, not aimless but purposefully following the Lord. Solomon said, "Obey the Lord! This is the beginning of knowledge."

With your purpose and priorities in focus, you can make every decision, knowing you're coming from a place of wisdom, and headed where you actually need to go, closer and closer to the Lord.

Turning to God and coming to know Him better is like having our ladder on the right tree.

Internalize this:

> **Let us fix our eyes on Jesus, the author and perfecter of our faith, who for the joy set before him endured the cross, scorning its shame, and sat down at the right hand of the throne of God.**

> **Hebrews 12:2**

I think the cafeteria was serving fish sticks that day. With fruit cup, if I remember correctly.

As their new teacher, I'd just sat down with my class of seventh graders, and was ready for a conversation that went no deeper than "Isn't pizza delicious?' or "I have a dog, do you?" If they asked any hard questions it might be, "Why do cats have whiskers?" or "Do we really need our pinky toes?"

Instead, this seventh-grade girl looked up at me and asked, "What's the worst thing you have ever done?" What?! I don't know that! I can't answer that! What do I say? Ask me about pizza, my dog, whiskers, or pinky toes! C'mon, ask me one of these. Or, at least give me multiple choice questions or true/ false. Not this one.

Now, I'd just graduated from seminary at the time. They didn't prepare me for questions like this! I think I still owed money to them. I figured we could just call it even. I managed to blurt out something about some foolish thing I'd done. But I knew that just wasn't the answer. And she gave me a disappointed look like, "No, that isn't it."

Now, I had learned over time to shoot straight with kids and give them answers when they asked. My non-answer wasn't that. So, later in the day, I decided to ask God the same question the little girl asked me. And wouldn't you know, it was one of those times that God answered. You know, in His way.

"The worst thing you have ever done was to keep Me out of your life," He answered. The opposite was logical – the best thing I have ever done was to welcome Christ into my life.

I realized too that this was not only the best thing I had ever done, but the best thing anyone could ever do.

Welcome Christ into your life and stay focused on Him if you haven't. Let all you do flow from this perspective. Have the right aim in life. Fix your eyes on Jesus.

Have your ladder on the right tree.

Reading: John 3:1-21

**"The most profound thing anyone has
ever done is follow the Lord."**

Day 16

Getting the Pew Poke
and Getting the Plank out of Your Eye

Sometimes one of the reasons we quarrel is simply because we are far too preoccupied on the faults of others.

For many of us, our lives would make a great shift if we became more focused on our own faults.

Jesus made this point in a particularly memorable way. He said, "Why do you look at the speck of sawdust in your brother's eye and pay no attention to the plank in your own eye?"

Oddly, whatever flaws we see in others really should seem like a mere speck compared to the plank in ourselves. If this is so, why would we be giving so much attention to the speck rather than the plank?

All of this focus on other's flaws makes it rather impossible to really build others up. After all, they're not too built up with us fixed on their speck. They are much more built up by us working on our plank.

Someone once said, "Be not angry that you cannot make others as you want them to be, since you cannot make yourself as you wish to be."

It makes total sense that we should focus on our own flaws. Our flaws are the ones we can do the most about. And when we do focus on our flaws instead of the flaws of others, there's a lot less useless quarreling and lot more personal responsibility.

Two really important things.

Internalize this:

> **How can you say to your brother, 'Let me take the speck out of your eye,' when all the time there is a plank in your own eye?**

> **Matthew 7:4**

The "Pew Poke". Ever gotten it?

If you're married, I bet you have. It's when your husband or wife pokes you during a sermon since what the pastor just said was obviously for them. The pastor says something like "Make sure you listen to others!" Poke comes in from wife to husband. Pastor says, "Give your spouse some space at times. Don't smother." Poke comes in from husband.

Now, it isn't limited to just husband or wife. The Pew Poke could come from mother to daughter, brother to sister. It really knows no bounds. Here's how it may have looked in the past. Pastor says, "Love your brother. Always look out for his good." Abel pokes Cain. Pastor says, "Believe God for the impossible." Abraham pokes Sarah.

Now this gets a little difficult if the husband or wife is in the choir. You have to stand up and yell over in this case, "Did you just hear that? Yeah. Good. That was for you. Write that down!" Well, that doesn't happen so much... outwardly but it does inwardly.

This is why I think there are some people who love doing the sound ministry in the church. And they do it for years on end without a single complaint about any of it. They don't complain about the equipment, new hard to follow technology, never-ending volume adjustment requests, nothing!

Why? They are far away from the Pew Poke, tucked safely into a sound booth that, to them, is like a barricade keeping them safe.

But why does it happen? Because we are often very preoccupied by the faults of others instead of our own.

Don't let it get like that for you. Be occupied with your own faults over others'. Hey, we all have plenty to be mindful of.

Avoid useless quarrels. Build others up.

Think of the plank, ignore the speck.

Reading: Romans 14

**"When it comes to faults,
think of your plank not their speck."**

Day 17

A Game Ball
and God's Plans for You

Most people have absolutely no idea how great God's will is for their life.

In fact, there are many people who think that if they follow God's will, they're gonna miss out on the good things of life.

Or, they live in a constant state of dread, walking on spiritual eggshells to avoid getting in trouble with God.

But His will is always the very best for us. The Creator loves us and knows exactly what His creation needs, and exactly how to get those things to us.

Instead of receiving from God, often we pull back thinking that somehow He doesn't actually have the best for us. We avoid what He wants for us instead of running toward it.

Some retraining of how we see God's will for us may completely transform how we live. It may lead us to stop running from His will and start wanting it above all else.

This would be the way to go since His plans are, in reality, far better than even the best we could come up with for ourselves.

His plans are glorious and wonderful and perfect!

Internalize this:

> **'For I know the plans I have for you,' declares the Lord, 'plans to prosper you and not to harm you, plans to give you hope and a future.'**
>
> **Jeremiah 29:11**

"Y'er OUT!"

A big game… for Little Leaguers. I'll never forget it. I'd gotten the last batter out in the field and my team won the game. I tossed the ball on the field somewhere and we all celebrated. One of my coaches came out to me right as we were wrapping up the round of high-fives, and asked where I'd put the ball.

Rats! I had no idea where the ball was. Now I'd done it. But I sure couldn't figure out why he was so desperate to get that ball. After all, we had others. We had lots. And this was a used one. All I could do was give him a rough idea of where I'd thrown it.

Then I tried to stay away from him.

He found the ball, and in front of the whole team gave it to me as a game ball – recognizing my achievement in getting the last batter out. He even wrote on the ball the achievement. He wanted me to have something wonderful.

And all along, I'd figured I was in trouble, the coach was mad at me, and it wasn't gonna go well. Really he just wanted to do something great for me. He wanted to give me a great memory. He wanted to celebrate what I had done.

Often it goes this way with God. He has something great for us and we seek to avoid Him, thinking the worst.

Know that the plans of God are great for you. They always are. They always will be. Believe that they always prosper you and not harm you; they bring a great hope and future.

Trust His plans. Let Him bring them all to pass in your life. Know it may not be easy things or things in just the same time frame we might be thinking of, but great things.

Know how much better it will go for you if you run to His will not from it at every turn.

Let God get those game balls to you.

Reading: Matthew 8:1-27

"Your view of God determines your response to Him."

Day 18

King Kong Couldn't Find Parking and Handling the Little Things Well

Sometimes how we handle the little things in life may be just as important as how we handle the big things.

The little things may be the training ground, the practice for those bigger things that are coming. When those bigger things come, how well we handled those little things may make all the difference.

David became assured that he would be able to defeat Goliath due to smaller victories that occurred before this. We are told he killed a lion and a bear protecting sheep before he encountered Goliath to protect Israel. David got his confidence in God from those little things. He said, "Your servant has killed both the lion and the bear; this uncircumcised Philistine will be like one of them." When he did those little things, no one saw and the consequences were much smaller. That would change.

Someone once said, "How we do anything is how we do everything." This would make the little things very important. It's the way promotion often takes place in the business world. You are given the bigger better jobs based only on how you did the smaller jobs.

The Bible also tells us that those who handle the little things are those who will handle the bigger things well too. It is all a reflection of our character, which is everything. Maybe in part it's why Jesus says that "Whatever you do to others you do to me".

Little is big.

Internalize this:

> **Whoever can be trusted with very little can also be trusted with much, and whoever is dishonest with very little will also be dishonest with much.**

> **Luke 16:10**

Save that spot!

I tried to park one day in New York City. Have you ever tried that? It's not easy. I think it's a design flaw of the city or something… they forgot to put in parking.

It's enough to make you angry and turn you into a hairy beast. In fact, I have a little theory about King Kong. I think he was not really a giant ape. No, I think he was just a guy who couldn't find parking in the city. He freaked out and turned into a hairy beast.

Yup, he is actually just a tourist from the Midwest where there is plenty of parking, wondering what to do with his car. He is late and had been driving in circles for hours. The woman he is holding as he swats planes atop the Empire State Building is his wife. If you listen real close, she is saying, "I told you we should've taken the subway!"

Godzilla? Just a guy who can't parallel park. Rode around in circles for hours. Started breathing fire.

So, how well do we do in our hearts when looking for parking? How well do we do with someone who took a spot we were about to take? How well do we do with our spouse during the whole search? How 'bout with God? How about all these "little" things?

How do we respond to people just in everyday life? How about with people who cannot repay us for our little acts of kindness? How about the little things we do when no one is looking?

Take these as the training ground, the character developers and revealers. So, count them as big too. Count them as your lion and your bear. They will prepare you and make you better at handling just about everything.

Be trusted with the little so you will be trusted with much.

Know that it is then you will defeat your goliaths too.

Reading: 1 Samuel 17:1-51

"Little things in life are big."

Day 19

Over the Hill at Thirty-One and Being the Right Age to Minister

We are meant to be in ministry at every age.

There is not a time where we're too young to contribute or too old to have a lot to offer. We can always connect with others in meaningful ways.

We see that in the Bible. The many commands we have to be in ministry never say stuff like… "if you're old enough or unless you are too old for that". No.

So the Bible addresses the young and older always affirming what we can accomplish. To the older, Proverbs reads, "Gray hair is a crown of splendor; it is attained by a righteous life." Moses was 80 when he was just getting going in ministry at the burning bush.

To the young, Paul says to Timothy, "Don't let anyone look down on you because you are young, but set an example for the believers in speech, in life, in love, in faith, and in purity." Some of the apostles, it is estimated, were very young people when they were with Christ, late teens even.

When we are young we have to wait for lots of things in life. There are minimum ages to vote, to drive, to work a job and so forth. But there is not a minimum age on ministry.

When we are older, we may retire from a job or be finished with a certain sport too. But we don't retire from ministry.

Ministry is for the young and older.

Internalize this:

> **Always give yourselves fully to the work of the Lord, because you know that your labor in the Lord is not in vain.**
>
> **1 Corinthians 15:58**

You know, it shouldn't be but it is. Physically we reach our peak in life really early. After this early peak, our bodies start a slow decline.

So think about this. If you are an NFL player, you will reach the peak of your career at about the age of 25. If you make it to 30, you are one of the old guys on the team. People start looking to you for leadership since you are so 'old'. If you make it to 40, you're probably the placekicker.

It's kind of funny to hear one of the NFL players "retire" and give one of those teary retirement speeches they often give. They have worked hard. They have set some records. They led their team to success and now it's all over. They cannot physically do it anymore. The tears flow. I can get caught up in all that… yes. Until I realize the guy retiring is 31.

It gets worse. Ballerinas, gymnasts, and others like that are over the hill at about 19. They are graceful and capable on balance beams before then. After, that? Done. That balance beam? Very unbalanced. Those uneven bars? Way too uneven. I am definitely not into a retirement speech from a 19 year old either.

Even in many regular careers that aren't purely physical, sometimes your peak is somewhere at about 55 for the industry. After that, a business may start looking to replace you with young blood. They offer you a great early retirement package and hope you're out. Airline pilots are out at 60 by law.

So, it's important for us to see that this is not the case when it comes to ministry. For most of us, we are not peaking at 19, 31, 55, or even 60 in ministry.

Know that ministry can be great and powerful year in and year out no matter what age we are, young and older.

If you are young, it is time to start in ministry if you haven't. If you are older, never think the next year in ministry can't be a great year, your best yet!

Enter in and stay in ministry.

The time to peak in ministry is now.

Reading: Exodus 3

"The time to peak in ministry is now."

Day 20

Touching the Moon
and How to Parent Well

They watch and learn.

Ever stop just to realize the very big role as parents we really do have? There is almost no doubt that a parent has a bigger influence on the child than anyone else.

Think about this. Almost everything your kid does for the first time they do with you or with your input or with the desire for your approval. This is a great bond. You matter so much in the life of your children.

That's why our lives should be what they ought to be. Our kids are looking at our lives. They will come to model much of what we do or do not do.

All the fundamentals of good parenting are already given in God's Word. Here are some of those principles:

> Love your children. Model the right behavior for your children.
> Guide, discipline, and encourage your children. Love your spouse.
> Acquire wisdom. Be gentle, self-controlled. Show goodness and kindness.
> Be active in ministry. Read the Bible and pray with them.
> Have an active church life. Love God above all else.

Live the things of the Bible out well and you fill the role of parent out well too. Ignore the things of the Bible and you will see that may show up in the life of your children too.

So, while the Bible is not just a manual on parenting, it isn't anything less either.

Internalize this:

The righteous man leads a blameless life; blessed are his children after him.

Proverbs 20:7

Touching the moon?

Our influence as parents hit me one day with my daughter. We were looking at the moon. It was the first time we looked at it and talked about it together. One of those many firsts with my children.

We talked about things like how the moon gets its light by reflecting the sun. How you can see the craters from here, that there have been men on the moon. She was fascinated.

But then it got even more interesting. She looked at me and asked if she could go on my shoulders. I put her up and saw her reaching for the sky. I wondered what she was doing at first. Then I realized it. She thought that maybe if she got on my shoulders, she would be able to reach that moon and touch it if she just stretched out far enough.

Just how big did she think I was?

The truth is we are really big in the eyes of our children. To them, you can do almost anything. I was her dad and it was nothing for me to get her to the moon. I wondered what else she thought I could do, like have her orbit the earth by spinning her by her arms, or grabbing Saturn's ring and giving it to her as a necklace.

While we as parents may not actually be able to do any of those things, we sure can provide our children with a loving nurturing and godly upbringing, using that big influence.

Look, no parent is perfect. That is understood… cut yourself some slack if you feel overwhelmed out there.

On the other hand, hold all the qualities the Bible calls you to as your goals every day and seek to meet those goals. Create a wonderful home. Know your children will be blessed after you.

Know it's even bigger than providing the moon.

Reading: Romans 12:9-21

"You are bigger in the eyes of your kids then you will ever know."

Day 21

Procrastination on the Golf Course and Procrastination in Life

Putting stuff off? Everyone does it – getting to the dentist for a cleaning, returning last Thursday's DVD, balancing your checkbook. No matter who you are, there are probably things you procrastinate about.

Ever notice how we can find just about any excuse to avoid these things too? We get interested in anything else. "Look at that spider make a web!" For some people, what's being put off is a lot more important than just having sparkling white teeth or avoiding late fees on a movie.

They're putting off receiving Christ, until later. They're putting off dealing with a pet sin, until later. They're putting off using their God-given talents to bless others, until later. They're putting off forgiving someone, until later.

By putting things like this off for "later", we may miss out on some of the greatest blessings and opportunities. We may be wasting a portion of our life. It's not like we mean to miss out or do harm; it's more like the old saying goes…

… "The road to hell is paved with good intentions."

Internalize this:

> **Be very careful, then, how you live – not as unwise but as wise, making the most of every opportunity, because the days are evil.**
>
> **Ephesians 5:16**

I couldn't believe when I read a certain golf course's policy on ball hawking. Ball hawking is when you go onto a golf course or range and take the balls that are there.

It's dangerous, it's distracting, and it's also stealing! So courses and ranges really don't like it. But… you'd barely know it from this course's ball hawking policy. Here it is (and my comments are in parentheses) .

1. First Offense: Request by the Ranger to discontinue ball hawking.
(Fair enough, but notice it's just a "request" and nothing will happen to you as a result.)

2. Second Offense: Request by the Golf Professional to discontinue ball hawking.
(Okay, now they're bringing in the big guns, the golf professional. He is not some hacker. He can play and now he's "requesting" that you stop.)

3. Third Offense: Form letter from the General Manager quoting the rules.
(I like how they went out of the way to tell you that this is only a form letter you will be given. No actual thought was put into it. Still nothing happens to you.)

4. Fourth Offense: Letter from the President of the Board of Directors.
(By now everyone knows you on the golf course by name. They say "Hi" to you and everything. It is your fourth offense and what happens… just another letter.)

5. Fifth Offense: Suspension of golf privileges for a period of two weeks.
(At this point you have so many balls from ball hawking that you are repaving your driveway with them and the only thing that happens to you is you can't golf for two weeks. Plus, this may be good – time to try another course.)

6. Sixth Offense: Suspension of all common area for a period of two weeks.
(Common area? What is that, the water fountain? You have been caught six times and all that happens is you can't have a sip of water. What will they say if you do drink, "Hands on your head. Back slowly away from the water fountain! Spit out that water you just took!"? And, they won't say that. After all, they know your name. They say, "Hi"!)

7. Seventh and Subsequent Offenses: Length of suspension for use of all common area will be determined by the Board of Directors.
(So now you can't have a sip of water for three weeks and it took a board to determine that.)

Pretty silly, huh? So, where does it show up in our life? Determine not to waste even another moment of your life. Make the most of every opportunity.

Reading: Romans 6:1-14

"What you can accomplish may be determined by what you refuse to put off."

Day 22

Throwing a Watch in a Lake
and Knowing God is Good

"God is great, God is good. Let us thank Him for this food."

This was the prayer we said before meals when I was a child. Maybe you prayed something similar. I only realize now that "good" and "food" don't actually rhyme. But, that's okay.

Seems like a very basic truth – God is good. It's something we intuitively know as kids as we pray prayers like that. Yet it's also something that many, many come to doubt when trouble or hardship hits. In fact, perhaps the most asked question of all time is "Why would a good God allow that (fill in the problem) to happen?" The simple truth that God is good from the prayer gets lost.

The reality is, we don't always know why trouble comes. We may never know why a certain hard thing happened. God's ways are higher than ours. We can think of a few reasons why God allows trouble. Often hardship causes us to grow more deeply in Him. The roots of a tree sink much deeper in the ground during a drought. They have to go deeper to find water. The tree is stronger as a result – but only after the hardship.

Going through trouble often makes us better qualified to help others. The cancer survivor is the first person we want to talk to if we are diagnosed, too.

Of course, trouble could lead someone to saving faith in Christ. It would all be well worth it if someone's eternal destiny is changed as a result.

There's also simply free will. Bad things happen because God allows choice not because He isn't good.

In the end, there is always a purpose that God is after by allowing hardship whatever that purpose might be. So when hardship hits, we can think of this purpose and know the simple prayer was right all along.

God is good.

Internalize this:

> Taste and see that the Lord is good; blessed is the man who takes refuge in him.
>
> Psalm 34:8

Hold on! Canoeing can be fun. But, there are a few things you gotta know. One is, just remember as you row out, you will usually have to row back that exact same amount! The rowing back may not be as fun! Here's another. Be sitting down when rough water comes your way.

Here's a case in point on that second one. Once, when I was a kid, I borrowed my mother's watch as a friend and I went out canoeing. My mother said before I left, "Don't throw it in the water." I thought, "Now why would I do that?" Her watch was safe. Right? But, since it was a ladies watch and also small, I didn't put it on, just held it while we were out on the canoe. Without expecting it, some rough water came upon us. The first thing I did? Throw my mother's watch in the lake.

Her words echoed in my mind, "Don't throw it in the water." (Add echo effect here.) Then shortly after, my words echoed in my mind, "Now why would I do that?" (Echo effect.) All this as the watch went to the bottom of the lake. My friend and I got in the water to try to retrieve it. That is, until a passer-by informed us of the large amount of snakes that may be in that water. You never saw two people get out of water so fast.

All this because I wasn't ready for some rough water along the way. And in life, getting thrown by some rough water happens all the time. We get thrown by troubles and blame God. We forget that He is good.

Be ready when trouble comes. Know that God has a purpose for the trouble, even though we may never know what that is. So, through it all, through each and every trial, get back to that understanding we knew as a child.

God is good.

Reading: Psalm 107 and Job 42:1-17

"We don't need to know the reason God has for a difficult thing – we just need to know He knows."

Day 23

Crashing a Super Bowl
and Crashing Church Life

But I go to church…

It's possible to go your whole life attending church and never actually become a Christian. Many people do it.

The reason is that there is a great distinction between attending church and actually knowing God personally. There is a distinction between knowing God exists and actually accepting Christ into our lives.

What we need to do in our lives is not just try to be a better person or more religious by attending church. Rather, we must seek to become a transformed person by coming to know God.

We do that by choosing to turn from our sin and receive Jesus Christ into our hearts. He receives all who welcome Him in. It is then we are right with God and have truly turned to Him.

Then church is no longer the empty ritual, good work, or thoughtless obligation it is for so many. It is then church comes to be what it ought to be, to better our relationship with God and give glory to Him.

It is then we are not just part of the churchgoing community but part of the actual body of Christ…

… just where we are really called to be.

Internalize this:

> **Yet to all who did receive him, to those who believed in his name, he gave the right to become children of God.**

> **John 1:12**

Ed "Skipper" Mcknally is famous in NFL football.

"Why? As a player? As a coach? Did he set some records? Did he lead his team to the Super Bowl?" Nope, absolutely none of those things.

In fact, he didn't play or coach a single down. No, Skipper Mcknally was famous simply for crashing Super Bowls, NFL parties, and other NFL events making himself appear as an insider when really he was very much not. He did it many times.

The most famous time was in Super Bowl IV in New Orleans between the Minnesota Vikings and the Kansas City Chiefs. Here it is believed that he put on a Vikings jacket and directed the team bus to where it needed to go. He then followed the team and sat with them on the sidelines… during the Super Bowl!

Towards the end of the game, it became apparent that the Chiefs were actually going to win. So Mcknally put on a Chiefs jacket and went over to the other side. When the Chiefs won, there is actual footage of him even helping to carry Chief's victorious coach Hank Stram off the field.

Nope, he never played a down, but there he was right in the middle of that great celebration. There are many people like that in church life. They are there. They are even doing the church equivalent of directing the team bus and carrying the coach off the field.

They are present and active but have never actually made a decision for Christ. They are not actually a part of the body of Christ. They have not accepted Christ yet. They know about Him but do not know Him.

Realize the incredible difference between going to church and knowing God… between knowing about Him and knowing Him. Realize the difference between trying to lead a better life and having a transformed life because Christ is in it!

Know that unless you have made an actual decision to accept Christ, you are not yet right with God through Christ and have not been transformed in Him.

Do not just crash church life! Receive Christ and become His child.

Reading: Hebrews 1:1-2:4

"There is a great gap between knowing God and knowing about Him."

Day 24

Missing Every Note
and Finding Unconditional Love

Unconditional love may be a bit hard to find out there.

Most love we experience (and give) has a lot of conditions built into it. Conditional love is the way most people 'love'. It says, "I will love you IF you make me feel good, do something for me, love me." Or something like that.

Jesus talked about this kind of love in very negative terms. He said "If you love only those who love you, what credit is that to you? Even sinners love those who love them."

This is not the kind of love we're meant to have for others and not the kind God has for us. He loves us without condition. We see this in how Jesus went to the cross loving us even while we were His enemies.

So, God calls us from any form of conditional love, to the love we must have, unconditional. This is what He means when He says, "Love one another as I have loved you." This love is what people yearn for, desperately need, and what they will respond most positively to.

Conditional love is really just using others, not loving them. They don't need this "love" and will not respond positively to it. They get this all the time.

They need unconditional love.

Internalize this:

> **But God demonstrates his own love for us in this: While we were still sinners, Christ died for us.**

> **Romans 5:8**

Music recitals when you are a kid can be pretty intimidating. I found this out the hard way.

One day, my family and another family got together and had our own music recital. Both families were pretty big so with just the two together, we had an instant audience. Several of us played an instrument so, instant recital too.

It was my turn to go and play the sax. Now my nerves really got in the way. So much so I could not really form my mouth the way it ought to for even one note to come out. It's fairly normal to miss a note here or there for any musician, particularly at my age. But I didn't miss a note. I missed them all.

Now I did manage a few squeaks and squeals, but they don't count as notes, I don't think. The families waited. I still couldn't get even one note out. It probably was only like a minute or two of me trying. But I can tell you that on that night, it felt like an hour or more went by of squeaks.

Now, I wish I could tell you that suddenly I got it all together and performed like there was no tomorrow, and I'm writing about this decades later because of the rousing performance and standing ovation that followed. No.

No standing ovation or rousing performance. I tell you I really did miss every note! But the families looked on and were as patient with me as could be. In fact, to my surprise as a very young person, they seemed to love me and respect me absolutely no less from it. They seemed to love and respect me as if I had hit every note.

No one got a song from me that night but I got to see what unconditional love looks like. I got a glimpse of how God sees us, the unconditional love He always has.

We mess up in life all the time and may wonder if God still loves us. Know He loves you the same even if you miss every note. Know that He loves you the same because the performance or lack thereof is not what makes Him love you in the first place. He loves you for you – always has, always will. His love is unconditional. Receive that love and give it to others that way too.

As if they hit every note.

Reading: Romans 8:28-39

**"Unconditional love everyone needs.
Conditional love everyone can do without."**

Day 25

An Uncomfortable Breakfast
and the Importance of Self-discipline

I've found that behind the greatest acts and accomplishments and right things done has always been self-discipline.

That is, the kind of self-discipline where you willingly give up immediate gratification for a greater return in the future. In a way, this would be forethought in action.

And, being undisciplined would be a lack of forethought in action. It seems to always cost us in the long run. Being undisciplined is a commitment to the immediate gratification at the expense of a future much greater gain.

Self-discipline can show up with how we are at work. The most disciplined seem to get ahead much faster. It shows up with school. Disciplined students succeed. It shows up in relationships. Disciplined people create deeper more lasting relationships. And we will need it to live holy, trust God, and be effective in ministry.

The Bible says, "Be self-controlled, upright, holy, and disciplined." Esau, in an undisciplined moment, gave up his birthright for a single meal since he was hungry. The Bible called him "godless".

When self-discipline overcomes lack of discipline, it always gets us ahead, always moves us forward, always rewards us so well. No wonder it's listed in the qualifications for church leaders. "He must be hospitable, one who loves what is good, who is self-controlled, upright, holy and...
... disciplined."

Internalize this:

> **For the grace of God has appeared that offers salvation to all people. It teaches us to say "No" to ungodliness and worldly passions, and to live self-controlled, upright and godly lives in this present age.**

Titus 2:11-12

Quick, hide!

One day, my brother decided to skip school. He and some friends got in a car and drove off to a diner.

As my brother was about to order, he could see that our father was also in the diner at the other end. "Oh no! I chose the wrong diner!" my brother must've thought.

He seriously hoped our father didn't see him. Now diners where we lived served every food that existed. So, they had huge menus. My brother became very thankful for that big menu – he used it as a shield to hide behind.

Now quite in contrast to my brother on that day, our father always went to work. In fact, in his 35 plus years of working, I don't recall that he ever took a sick day.

He would always be up getting his tie and suit on and going to work. I never really knew what he did at work, mind you. But I did know he went and did it – whatever 'it' was.

So, my brother kept hiding behind that menu until our father came up to the cashier and paid his bill and left. My brother was very relieved, ate his breakfast and went up to pay about a half hour later figuring he was in the clear.

But, the cashier quickly told my brother that his bill and the bill of his friends was paid by a guy that left about 30 minutes ago.

Oh no!

I remembered that time since it was in my mind, discipline meeting undisciplined, and discipline winning as it always does.

Lead a self-controlled life and win too. See how discipline gets you a better job, better relationships, productive ministry, and a deeper walk with God.

Practice forethought in action.

Reading: Titus 1:1-9

"Self-discipline is forethought in action."

Day 26

Golf Balls for Lunch
and How God Provides

Worry is not a good thing for your life. In fact, actually, it's terrible.

It's not much fun, of course – but beyond that, it does something to you spiritually. The Bible says that worry chokes the Word within us and makes us less fruitful.

God goes further with this, and explains that there's really no reason for worry either. He assures us of a couple things: He'll provide for our needs and He knows exactly how to do that.

There's this whole discussion in the Bible about eggs and scorpions, where God assures us that He knows the difference, and that we don't have to worry about Him pulling a switch. You get what is best for you, eggs, not what you don't need, scorpions.

Christ said, "Now suppose one of you fathers is asked by his son for a fish; he will not give him a snake instead of a fish, will he? Or if he is asked for an egg, he will not give him a scorpion, will he?"

Worry is a way of essentially limiting God, blocking yourself from receiving everything He wants to bring your way. Worry is like closing a container that God wants to fill.

He calls us to trust and hope in Him instead. His providence is so great.

We never need to worry.

Internalize this:

> **Those who hope in the Lord will renew their strength. They will soar on wings like eagles; they will run and not grow weary, they will walk and not faint.**
>
> **Isaiah 40:30-31**

Look out for the crows!

As part of the golf classes I taught, we'd go hit balls in a grassy field, far from cars and houses. It started with one or two crows, but I guess word got out, because it became a pretty regular occurrence. These birds would swoop down onto the field and steal the balls we were hitting.

The supervisor at the Park, tasked with keeping track of our inventory, finally called me in. This was going to be interesting.

"Um, there are these giant crows… and they kinda swoop down, get golf balls in their beaks, and take off with them. I don't know, maybe they think they're eggs or something." This sounded crazy even to me.

I got the look. The look that says I could just as easily have told her that leprechauns leapt out of the woods and danced around and then took all our balls putting them in shiny green pails. She sent me back outside, shaking her head. Yet it was true.

And I thought I was getting the bad end of the deal. But imagine how the baby birds felt when they got a golf ball instead of an egg for lunch that day. Golf balls are made pretty well these days, lots of distance and good feel for putting… but none are good for breakfast, I'm sure.

Know that God's giving is nothing like that. He always provides brilliantly and perfectly in every situation we ever face. Know that when we need an egg, we get an egg not a golf ball.

In fact, we get far beyond anything we could even ask, think, or imagine. That's the kind of God you can trust.

Here's a big choice we all need to make: Replace worry with trust and peace and joy as you wait on the Lord.

And get all those eggs!

Reading: Luke 11:1-13

**"You simply can't worry and trust God
at the same time."**

Day 27

Adam and Eve's First Date and How to Have a Great Marriage

"I do!"

One of the most influential things going on in your life is probably your marriage.

A good marriage is an amazing thing. It has a ripple effect out to every other area of your life. You are different with your career. You are different in every other relationship. You are different in your relationship with God – all based upon how it's going in your marriage. No wonder the Bible calls us to have absolutely wonderful marriages.

These are marriages where there's great love and encouragement flowing person to person. There's great admiration and mutual respect. There's a sense of walking through life together with joyful support of one another.

Wonderful marriages exist when both spur one another on to deeper things with the Lord. These are marriages where the welfare of one another is watched carefully; where service to each other is put above self. You live as "one" just as the Bible declares you to be.

And, even the most difficult marriages can be made to be wonderful by God. Nothing is too difficult for Him. There's never a need to give up if it's not right, but to give it to God. And all marriages need work. You never coast. You always look to improve. Good marriages must always be made better.

If you love God with all you are and you have a great marriage, you're pretty much on top of the world!

Internalize this:

> **He who finds a wife finds what is good and receives favor from the Lord.**
>
> **Proverbs 18:22**

Mark Twain once noted that Adam and Eve had it easy – everything they said was original. As a writer, he would appreciate that!

Well, Adam also had it easy when it came to getting together with Eve. I mean there were not like thousands of people to choose from. There was just Eve and there was just Adam. All he had to say was, "Well, seeing as we are the only two people, I suggest we get together." Done.

Adam couldn't blow this like guys often do. He didn't even need any of those cheesy pick-up lines. They wouldn't have worked anyway. He couldn't be like, "Hello, you are the only woman in the world to me." But of course.

And Eve couldn't do the whole hard to get thing. She couldn't say, "Well, we'll see". Or, even that famous line that many have uttered, "I wouldn't go out with you unless you were the last person on earth", wouldn't have worked.

The whole dating thing would go much smoother too. Adam wouldn't have to be like, "Does she like me? What are her girlfriends saying? Is it too early to call her again? I don't want to look overly eager." Eve would not have to change her clothes five times before a date, well fig leaves.

The online dating services couldn't fail either. Adam could put he likes rhinoceroses and pickles, is seven feet tall, and has a Mohawk. Up comes Eve. Eve puts she likes unicorns and pudding, never leaves the house. Up comes Adam.

They knew they were meant for each other since they were the only two people. But, you can know that too about the husband or wife you have. God has put you together. You were meant for each other as if you were the only two people on earth.

Live like it. Make your marriage work. Make your marriage great. Let that ripple effect from a good marriage go out to your careers, your other relationships, and your relationship with God.

Love your mate… and know it's a good thing you have found!

Reading: Genesis 2:4-24

"The spouse you have is the perfect one for you."

Day 28

A Message to Garcia
and Spreading the Gospel Message

We have a message to get out to all the world.

Does this excite you? It should. The message we happen to have is the greatest message we could possibly have. It's the message of the death and resurrection of Jesus Christ.

We know it's our message and our duty to get it to all the world. Jesus told us so. We are given all kinds of encouragement to get this message to others. Here are a few:

We are told Christ tells is with us always.
We are told how ready people are for the message.
We are told people need to hear the message.
We are told that God will get results.
We are told how simple the message is.

The question is, how well are we doing at getting this message to where it needs to go? Have we actually taken it and circulated it to the people in our lives?

The greatest thing we could do for someone perhaps is to tell them of Christ. Our passion for others and Christ should lead us to share the gospel.

And, go into all the world…

… and next door too.

Internalize this:

> **How beautiful on the mountains are the feet of those who bring good news, who proclaim peace, who bring good tidings, who proclaim salvation.**
>
> **Isaiah 52:7**

40,000,000 copies!

There is a famous writing that has been translated into all the major languages of the world. Over 40 million copies have been printed. It is called "A Message to Garcia" by Elbert Hubbard. It's a simple yet profound work about being a great messenger or employee or assistant of any kind. Businesses use it to train employees. It is a great training for all of life.

It talks about a young man named Rowan. He was summoned by his country to deliver a message to Garcia, a General somewhere in the mountain vastness of Cuba. The message was critical yet, in that day, no mail or telegraph could reach the General.

As the account goes, this is what Rowan did: "[He] took the letter, and sealed it up in an oilskin pouch, strapped it over his heart, in four days landed by night off the coast of Cuba from an open boat, disappeared into the jungle." "In three weeks came out on the other side of the island, having traversed a hostile country on foot, and delivered his letter to Garcia."

The author then says, "The point I wish to make is this: Rowan [was given] a letter to be delivered to Garcia; Rowan took the letter and did not ask, 'Where is he at?' No. That was part of his duty. He would find where the General was at. He would be a great messenger."

It goes on to contrast Rowan to the way most employees or assistants respond to a task. Most grumble, try to get someone else to do it, say it isn't their job, wonder why it needs to be done, put off the task, do the job halfway, make excuses. Rowan got it done! (And so the book is a training tool!)

This is how we must be with the gospel. We have been given a message to deliver. Will we grumble, leave it for others, wonder why it needs to be done, put it off, do it halfway, make excuses… or will we get it done?

The article concludes that "The world cries for such [people like Rowan]: he is needed and needed badly – the man who can 'Carry a Message to Garcia.'"

Such is true of the one who will carry the gospel to the world.

Reading: Acts 2:22-41

"Be as great a messenger as the message we bring."

Day 29

Missing a Thumb
and Finding Purpose in All Things

As we go through life, it's so important to know that God has a purpose for what is going on in our lives.

Life is not going on by chance, randomness, or in a haphazard way though it may appear that way. God is behind it all.

The world is not like a clock that God set up to run by itself. Instead, He is involved in all things leading to a particular end as He pleases. It's quite the opposite of a clock.

So, the Bible says that God causes the rain that comes and every little bird that falls to the ground. Nothing, not even these seemingly random and small things, happen apart from God.

Matthew's Gospel says, "[God] sends rain on the righteous and the unrighteous." "Are not two sparrows sold for a penny? Yet not one of them will fall to the ground outside your Father's care."

This can be very helpful to us when something difficult happens. It was not by chance or by a God who does not care or is not involved. It occurred with Him over the event with some reason for it.

Knowing God is behind it all means so much to our level of trust in God, the gratitude we will show Him or not, the sense of purpose we will know exists.

All really important qualities for a godly life.

Internalize this:

[God] works out everything in conformity with the purpose of his will.

Ephesians 1:11

A story is told of a king who lived in Africa. He loved to shoot guns, getting target practice. The king had an assistant who went everywhere the king went and helped him. So, he helped with the king's target practice too. He would prepare the guns for fire and hand them to the king.

The assistant to the king had a phrase he would say a lot, especially when something bad happens. It was, "There's a reason."

One day the assistant handed a gun to the king and it mistakingly went off in the king's arms blowing off the top digit of his thumb. After helping get the king taken care of, the assistant later said, "There's a reason."

The king was infuriated, however. He said to his assistant, "There's no good reason for this. And, I am going to punish you. Off to jail with you!" So, off to jail the assistant went.

Some time passed and the king was out hunting alone when he ran into a tribe of cannibals. They saw the king as their next meal. He was terribly frightened. But, then the cannibals noticed the king was missing a part of his thumb. They were superstitious and could not eat a person unless he had all his parts. They let the king go.

The king was so elated that he rushed to the jail where he had put his assistant. He got him out of prison saying, "You were right! There was a reason! I am so sorry to have put you in jail all this time." The assistant predictably replied about the time he spent in jail, "There's a reason."

The king said, "No, I wronged you. What reason could there have been to be in jail?" The assistant said, "Simple. I have all my body parts and if I hadn't been in jail… I would have been with you!"

See the events of life in a different way. See that "There's a reason". Know God is behind it all. Reject the clock view of the world. Reject the chance view of things. Know He is even in control of the rain and birds, and everything else.

Trust Him and walk in gratitude and a sense of purpose for all things.

Know there is a reason.

Reading: Job 40:1-14

"There's a reason."

Day 30

Hallmark Cards You Don't Want
and Right Words You Do Want

Someone once said that if they could pick a super power, it would not be to be able to fly, or have x- ray vision, or incredible strength. It would just be to be able to say the right things at the right time.

The truth is, none of us have that superpower. We stumble over our words, we speak rashly. Often we don't know what to say or say too much. In fact, the Bible says in James, "The tongue also is a fire, a world of evil among the parts of the body." Hmm, the very opposite of a superpower.

The things we say must be chosen thoughtfully. They must be words that actually edify other people and make them better. We have all experienced words that hurt and words that heal. The old saying, "Sticks and stones may break my bones but words will never hurt me" simply is not true.

The Bible is quick to praise a person who watches what they say and says the right things. According to Proverbs, "A word aptly spoken is like apples of gold in settings of silver."

It is clearly possible to have just the right words and use these right words in powerful ways. So Proverbs also says, "Gracious words are a honeycomb, sweet to the soul and healing to the bones."

While it's no one's superpower to always say healing, edifying words, we sure can make it a big part of our life and our very high goal.

Internalize this:

> **Do not let any unwholesome talk come out of your mouths, but only what is helpful for building others up according to their needs, that it may benefit those who listen.**

> **Ephesians 4:29**

Hallmark writers: Your jobs are safe.

Yes. It's true that Song of Solomon is a love letter from Solomon to his fiancé and continues after they are married. But, you know what? I'm not sure Solomon actually knew how to give a compliment to her. You have met people like that too, I'm sure. They mean well but... like the guy who says something like, "You look less fat in that outfit." You know... that kind of guy.

So when you read Song of Solomon, here are a few of the nuggets he actually shared with his fiancé.

> "Your hair is like a flock of goats."
> "Your teeth are like a flock of newly shorn ewes."
> "Your neck is like the tower of David."
> "You are as awesome as an army."

Really? I don't think the goats and ewes stuff is working. Rarely is a comment about someone's neck a big winner. And, the whole army thing probably not a big hit with her. But this one is my favorite. He also said:

> "Your belly is like a heap of wheat."

Trust me. Any sentence to a woman beginning with the words "your belly" never ends well.

Now he insults those around her with this one... "Like a lily among the thorns, so is my darling among the maidens." Well, of course, those comments all had a different meaning in their day than what we are picking up on. They were actually compliments; the meaning clear then just not now.

But they may remind us of some of the rash and foolish words we have spoken and how hurtful they were. They may remind us of some of the very edifying words and how helpful they are.

Be thoughtful with what you say and use your words to speak what is good, what is true, what is edifying, what will benefit those who listen. Choose words that are healing to the bones, sweet to the soul... apples of gold.

Tame the tongue!

Reading: James 3:2-18

"Think twice, speak once."

Day 31

A Fourth Grade Graduation
and a Great Journey of Learning

Never done!

You know, the Bible tells us that we're never done learning. There is always so much more for us to know and see.

Unfortunately, many believers feel they have learned enough. They never go to Sunday School or read the Scriptures intently. Many say in their hearts, "No, I'm done."

Instead, what God has in store is so much more. He wants to take us on an incredible journey of exploring, discovering, seeing new and great things. Learning! This adventure is not to be missed. It's a call of God. And the things He has for us are so wonderful. Scripture says, "Acquiring wisdom is like sport to the wise."

Some call it a "beginner's mind". It means having this sense that no matter how much we know and have learned, we have a lot more to learn. This approach will yield so much for us.

Being a lifelong learner is a key to a heart increasing in wisdom day in and day out – being on the journey God has for us.

Just where we need to be!

Internalize this:

> **Open my eyes that I may see**
> **wonderful things in your law.**

> **Psalm 119:18**

"I demand my guidance counselor!"

I was a full-time student until I was 26. I love telling that to little kids. They look at me in horror and disgust. They shake their heads at me and think,

"I hope my life doesn't end up like yours." Or they say, "Dude, how many times did you fail? You should've done your homework."

Well, not only was I a student so long but I have found that after I got out, the real learning began. However, there was a time I thought I was done with schooling. It was at the end of the 4th grade. That's right, I knew how to read and do math so that was it. I was sure of it.

Now I had two older brothers and an older sister. They went on for more schooling. They were in the 7th, 9th, and 10th grades. Now if they needed more schooling, that's fine. I'm not judging them. Just glad I was done.

So, it was quite a shock to find that I was actually enrolled in the 5th grade. "There must be some mistake!" I thought. We must have a meeting with my parents and the Principal. You know, a little pow-wow, a little meeting-of-the-minds, a little getting-on-the-same-page thing here.

And I wanted my Guidance Counselor present. I'm not saying anything until she arrives. I know my rights. Legal Counselor, Guidance Counselor… same thing, right? Well, oddly enough, I actually did end up in the 5th grade. Can you believe that?

Unfortunately, that's the way it is in our hearts sometimes. We figure that, in a way, we're done. We have learned enough. All the while, it's more like we have just finished the 4th grade.

Go with God on that wonderful journey He has for you as your Shepherd, the journey of discovery after discovery, Him showing you more and more of what you don't know now.

Know there is so much more to learn. Be a lifelong learner of the things of God. Have a beginner's mind. Let learning be like a sport to you.

Find those wonderful things from God.

Reading: Psalm 119:1-24

"The best students never graduate."

Day 32

A Frisbee Cookie Gift
and the Indescribable Gift of Christ

What's the best gift you've ever given?

May need to think a while on that one. I have heard some good answers like, "The gift of myself" or "The gift of my children to the world."

But, by far the greatest gift you've ever been given is the gift of Jesus Christ. By this one gift every person who has ever lived has been given the opportunity to be right with God. Jesus died for our sins so that the penalty of our sin was paid in Him. Paul says, "Thanks be to God for His indescribable gift."

But here is the confusion about gifts. A gift must be received or you don't have it. You've got to actually accept the gift in order to call it your own. An elementary but overlooked point in this whole gift giving thing. In the same way, Christ must be received and then we experience all the benefits of this great gift: forgiveness, eternal life, knowing God.

So many just kind of ponder the gift of Christ, maybe admire it, maybe believe it exists, but they never open it. They never open their heart and receive – like leaving an unopened present.

Receiving is key.

Internalize this:

> **For it is by grace you have been saved,**
> **through faith – and this is not from yourselves,**
> **it is the gift of God – not by works,**
> **so that no one can boast.**

> **Ephesians 2:8-9**

It's okay. Just admit it. We're not always all that good at picking the right gifts for people.

It's why gift cards and cash are getting more and more popular. We gave up, bought the gift card, and everyone is happier. Even the Wise Men had their issues on gift giving. Gold, frankincense, myrrh… for a newborn? The one who gave gold is the guy who gave up and just went with cash!

My mom puts the receipt in with the gift now in case I want to take it back. I wonder if her next step, just to make it even easier, will be to buy the gift and then return it for me! There would just be a note saying, "I got you a gift and returned it for you. You have store credit. Just get there within 30 days. Happy birthday!"

I remember one time when I was dating. I decided to bake some cookies and give them as a gift. There was one big problem. The cookbook I was using simply said "Add the appropriate amount of flour."

Wait a minute! Did it say "Appropriate amount"? What is the appropriate amount? I had no idea. Give me numbers… 1 cup… 2 cups! My need for preciseness became clear as the cookies baked. They got giant… almost the size of Frisbees. And, they were completely uncooked in the middle. So, they were cookies with a surprise in the middle… raw flour. Other cookies have caramel in the middle or cream. Not mine. The amount of flour I added was very inappropriate I can assure you of that.

Well, now as a joke, I put the cookies in a jar and put a bow on it. (Had to be a big, wide-mouth jar, of course!) I presented them and we had a good laugh. We could've gone out and had a good Frisbee throw.

Some gifts are like this in life. Not so good. But realize the greatness of the gift of Jesus. And realize it is just like other gifts… it must be received. If you have never let Him in your life, do it.

It's a simple decision to welcome Him in and receive Him as your Lord, as simple as receiving any other gift. You open your heart and let Him in. Know how important the opening part is to gift giving.

Open the greatest gift.

Reading: John 10:7-18

"There are good gifts, bad gifts, and the greatest gift – Jesus Christ."

Day 33

The Worst Golf Shots
and Handling Failure Well

How well do you fail?

One of the greatest keys to success is not how well you handle success or how competent you are, but how well you handle failure. Do you let it stop you? Do you fear it so much that you don't even start something? Do you avoid constructive feedback?

These are the responses of many, many people to failure. It kind of all comes down to your perspective on failure – what you tell yourself about yourself when you fail.

What if, instead of letting the prospect of failure keep you from moving forward, you recognized failure as sort of a (twisted!) gift? In failure, you give yourself an opportunity for further learning – and what you learn will serve you in the future, if you let it.

Tomas Edison said that he failed 1,000 times for every one invention. He made 1,093 inventions. Taken literally, he failed over a million times along the way.

Anyone calling him a failure? No. Anyone think of him for the million misses? No. In fact he said he didn't fail any of those times really. He just invented another way that didn't work.

Anyone who's ever accomplished anything great likely has a long, long string of failures leading up to that success.

They just failed well!

Internalize this:

> **Create in me a pure heart, O God,**
> **and renew a steadfast spirit within me.**

> **Psalm 51:10**

I think I may have witnessed three of the worst golf shots ever made.

Shot #1: Give that goose a helmet.
One guy I played with hit a goose with his ball. He hit the ball so low that even though the goose was far away, he nailed it.

Did you know geese can make really loud noises? They can. We joked with the guy saying, "Hey, we're golfing, not hunting."

Shot #2: Why you may want a helmet yourself.
Another guy once hit his ball so far off to the side that it hit the marker telling him what hole he was on. This marker is just off to your right or left or even behind you when you start the hole.

The ball ricocheted off the marker and went backward, almost hitting the rest of us who were playing with him. He started the hole about 350 yards away. For his second shot, he was 400 yards away.

Shot #3: Why you may need a change of clothes.
I once shot a ball that was on the edge of the water. The shot seemed to go off okay. But, I looked over at my playing partner to find he was covered in mud from my shot. It's one thing to get a little muddy from your own shot. But this? Poor guy.

Look, you're going to have days and times and decisions that just plain stink - like these golf shots. It's all part of life.

Commit yourself to learning from your mistakes and always getting better. Learn how to bounce back, and you may even amaze yourself by what you ultimately accomplish.

Add a great deal of patience to everything you do too.

Like Edison.

Like all who eventually succeed!

Reading: Psalm 51

"Success often comes with a thousand errors behind us."

Day 34

Winning a Marathon at the Age of 61 and Trusting the Perfect Timing of God

Sometimes we have so much trouble with God's timing of things.

Perhaps we need results now. "It's taking too long." Then there are things we wish could wait. "It's happening too fast." Whatever we say, our trouble is with God's timing.

He comforts us many times in the Bible assuring us He is aware of the timing. Peter said, "The Lord is not slow in keeping his promise, as some understand slowness." The psalmist adds, "He who watches over you will not slumber."

God commands us to use time well – another way of assuring us that He himself uses time well. "[Make] the most of every opportunity, because the days are evil."

God had the timing perfect for Christ's dying for our sins. Paul said, "At the right time Christ died for the ungodly."

He has the perfect timing for everything…

… even though sometimes things may seem to be going too fast

… and sometimes things may seem to be going too slow.

Internalize this:

> **The Lord is not slow in keeping his promise, as some understand slowness. Instead he is patient with you, not wanting anyone to perish, but everyone to come to repentance.**

2 Peter 3:9

I always thought a marathon was about 25 miles long – almost exactly 24 ½ miles too long for me.

But, in Australia they have an ultra-marathon that is 543.7 miles long, Sydney to Melbourne. It takes some five days to complete. Can you believe that?

Even more bizarre is that it was once won by an older farmer named Cliff Young. He set a record time of it in 1981 at the age of 61.

Many of the other runners with him were world-class. They had years of training behind them and Nike and Addidas endorsements. Most were under 30.

But 61 year-old Cliff Young won.

People wondered why this farmer was entering the race all. They thought it was a joke as he showed up in boots and overalls. And, when the race started, Cliff did fall way behind the other runners. That would change.

As each day passed, the other runners would stop to sleep a few hours each day. Not Cliff. He never slept. With each passing day, he caught up a little more to the front of the pack before surpassing them all by Day 5.

By not sleeping, he mastered time and won. He became a bit of an Australian hero after all this.

Know that God is a master of time too.

Know that nothing occurs in your life with undue haste or undue delay – no matter how it may feel at the time.

Know God never slumbers either, like Cliff, and accomplishes everything with perfect timing.

Trust God for the timing of all things. Know He always does everything at the…

… right time.

Reading: Romans 5:1-11

**"Let the Master of Time
master it in your life."**

Day 35

A Plea to the Sports Editor
and Having Great Motive for Prayer

What's your favorite sound?

Tough question.

There are lots of good sounds. You might like the sound of classical piano, of a forest of birds in the morning, of steady ocean waves at night.

These are all good. But none of these is my favorite sound. My favorite sound is the sound of the voice of my children.

Yes, that is rich, deeply moving, and better than anything else.

I started to think, if this is how I feel, maybe it's the same with God! Maybe He is counting the sound of my voice (and all His children) as His favorite sound!

If so, then the doctrine of adoption, which says that when we receive Christ we become His child, has great significance for prayer.

It would be why He delights to hear our prayer and always listens! It would be why God refers to our prayers as "incense" and a "soothing aroma"!

No wonder we are meant to pray so much.

Internalize this:

Pray constantly.

1 Thessalonians 5:17

Ever write to the editor?

I did once with the same sort of urgency that many people write to the editor of a paper.

However, I didn't write to the general editor, just the sports editor. I was not an angry adult or anything either, just about six years old. I found out that the sports editor was retiring.

Now, at six years old, I didn't even know what retirement really meant. I never held a job, so I certainly didn't know what it meant to stop doing a job. I thought maybe retirement was like dying or quitting. I had no idea that it was maybe just the next phase of life for someone.

So I wrote to the sports editor whose nickname was "Legs" and begged him to have more sense than to retire. "Please stay!" my little letter basically said in a full page worth of my six year old handwriting.

Well, Legs was so touched by my letter, that he printed the whole page just as I wrote it on the back page of the paper.

That is a pretty impressive response to someone who is just six. I was touched! My parents were shocked!

I never found out whether or not he retired but his response to my letter, treating it as so important and welcomed, was enough for me. I still remember seeing my handwriting on that back page.

This is a picture of how God responds to our prayers. They mean a lot to Him! He puts them in the paper filling the back page, so to speak.

Count your prayers to God in this way. Know they mean so much to God.

Let the soothing aroma that they are, rise up to Him.

Know that, just maybe, God's favorite sound…

… is your voice.

Speak to Him!

Reading: Matthew 26:36-46

"Lack of motive for prayer shows a lack of understanding about prayer."

Day 36

Surviving NASCAR Crashes
and Surviving Every Trial

"All things"?

When you're going through something tough, it's comforting knowing that it's all going to work out just fine because God is in control.

That's why one of the all-time favorite verses in the Bible is Romans 8:28, about God working everything for your good. Yes. All things!

What an empowering and wonderful promise to know God can and will do that. That all things bad that happen in our lives will be transformed to something good by God. Nothing is happening in vain and may make us infinitely better instead. God will make it so by what He does with it all.

Ever notice how people who have had a tragedy happen become much more able to help people in similar situations? Ever notice how much more capable you are at almost anything after you survive a trial?

Notice no one actually escapes trials and tribulations? We all have something, big or small, to go through.

And we can remember as we see these trials, that God is at work, using the trials every time in the life of the believer...

... working all things to the good.

Internalize this:

> **And we know that in all things God works for the good of those who love him, who have been called according to his purpose.**

> **Romans 8:28**

Just another fireball!

What amazes me most about NASCAR racing is how these guys can have such severe accidents and just get up and walk away. The car does like three or four flips, is completely crushed, set on fire and everything else, and the driver comes out of the accident just fine. They remove their helmet, brush themselves off, and go home.

I even saw one guy get out and go over to another driver and yell at him. No, he wasn't concerned about the fireball he just stepped out of but the rudeness of that other racer really got to him.

What do they say to their wives at the dinner table? "Ah, had a major, major accident again today. Car blew up into a giant fireball. No, I'm fine." Same conversation next week too.

Now they say that's got something to do with super special stuff they do to the cars to make them so much safer. About that – hey, how about whatever they're doing to those cars, do it to mine, too! I want that. You get into a giant five-car pile-up and everyone's just brushing off their clothes.

Instead, with our cars, it's like you get into a tiny fender-bender and three paramedics are all over you telling you to not look toward the light.

Just as they go through many of those crashes without a scratch, we can go through life's trials without a scratch, too, coming out of them even better. Realize the greatness of our God to be able to work everything together for the good.

Trust Him that there is something great coming from all the little inconveniences, tragedies, and everything in-between.

Know that when you do, you'll walk away from life's fireballs unscathed and better for it…

… with everything worked to the good.

Reading: James 1:1-12

"God works all things together for the good."

Day 37

Christmas Decorations in April and Having a Steady Walk with God

Some things are meant to last forever – but others are practically disposable. It's really important to know the difference.

The thing that is meant to be most permanent is your abiding faith in the Lord Jesus Christ. This is not the place for an on-again, off-again relationship. It's not something to be while you're at church, but not at work or home. It is not something you do when others are looking and not when you're alone.

Consistency is one of the marks of true maturity in Christ. It's what follows when we have grown, become more like we are meant to be. Sure, there are dry times and mountaintop experiences for everyone, but the mature are consistent too.

When others look at your life, they expect to see this consistency. They know it's a part of a genuine walk with God. There is great joy and power in a consistency with God that grows stronger and stronger over time.

This is the kind of walk that is meant for you. This is the kind of walk with God that is meant for all.

Internalize this:

> **Preach the Word; be prepared in season and out of season; correct, rebuke and encourage – with great patience and careful instruction.**
>
> **2 Timothy 4:2**

Ever notice how you can do some things in the Christmas season you can't do the rest of the year? Try doing the same things in, say, July. Your neighbors will think you're crazy. Think about it. If you have your decorations up right after Thanksgiving, you are a punctual, great neighbor. If you have those very same decorations still up in April, you are a freaky, lazy, weird neighbor. Same decorations, mind you!

If a group of carolers comes to your house in December, your whole family rushes to the window to listen. You open the door and offer cookies. In August, you wonder why there is a pack of teens in the front yard. You close the shades and call the police. It could be the same kids!

If, in December, you get stopped by a cop for speeding and roll down the window and he hears "The First Noel" playing, he'll probably let you go with a warning and a "Merry Christmas". If he hears "The First Noel" in June after stopping you, you are pretty sure to get the biggest fine possible. You might even end up incarcerated, playing it on a harmonica.

Now all of this is totally confusing for kids. All year we tell kids to cut down on the sweets. "Eat fruits and vegetables instead," we say. Christmas time comes and we're baking cookies all day. We have red ones, green ones, different shaped ones and we say, "Eat up – I'll make more!"

Same thing with toys. All year we say, "No, you can't have that. No, not that either." Christmas time comes: "Make a list! Check it twice! I need to know what you want."

And what about the tree? I mean, is there any other time of the year where you want a dead tree in your house? At Christmas, you love your dead tree. You decorate it with lights and ornaments, garland, and even a star on top. You water it every day and turn it on and off. You put all your gifts under it.

Then, suddenly, just one week after Christmas, you can't wait to have that thing out of your house. You strip it of all the decorations and lights, ornaments, and star. You toss it to the curb and as it blows down the street yell, "Good riddance!"

Hey. Life's like that sometimes. There's a lot that's temporary. But your faith is not to be seasonal.

Commit yourself to a consistent walk with God, constant growth, and all the joy and power that comes with it.

Be ready, in season and out.

Reading: 1 Peter 1:13-25

"What we consistently value makes us who we are."

Day 38

Knocked off a Log
and Seeing God as He Really is

He's mean. He hates me. He's far from me. He wants to take all the joy out of my life.

May sound crazy to you – but there are millions of people walking around thinking just these thoughts about God.

Could be in part from some past experiences interpreted by us the wrong way. Many experiences we have end up giving us a heart picture of God – sometimes it's not accurate, but it's usually very powerful. With a negative picture of God, why would anyone be open to moving closer to Him?

The goal is to get to know God for who He actually is. He is loving, caring, and desires the very best for us. He's the one who loves you so much that He sent His only Son to die for you so you could be restored to Him.

He's the one who calls you 'friend', 'beloved', and 'child'. He's the one who really has your best in mind and knows just what that is.

Hey, we're all in need of having our view of God changed.

Internalize this:

> **Praise the Lord, my soul,**
> **and forget not all his benefits—**
> **who forgives all your sins**
> **and heals all your diseases,**
> **who redeems your life from the pit**
> **and crowns you with love and compassion,**
> **who satisfies your desires with good things**
> ** so that your youth is renewed like the eagle's.**

> **Psalm 103:2-5**

Ouch!

One day when we were kids, we were all outside playing baseball in a field. My little brother didn't really like sports, so he just stayed away from the game. Well, he tried to, anyway.

But, one day, he was way out in the woods walking on a fallen tree. All of the sudden, the batter hit the ball so far that it left the field and went into the woods on the fly. Of course… it hit my brother, knocked him right off the log. Now he really didn't like sports.

But beyond that, my brother knew the batter that hit him and for a long time after, was afraid to go near him. He just associated that batter with pain. Every time he saw him, in fact, he'd run the other way.

After a while the batter, who also was a kid, did something really wise. One day, when he saw my brother run away again, he called him over. My brother wouldn't go. But, a few other kids actually physically kept my brother from getting away.

Then when the two were close together, the batter whipped out of his pocket a stack of several unopened packs of baseball cards, complete with a stick of gum in each pack. Baseball cards were really the thing in that day. One by one, he opened each pack in front of my brother and then gave him all the cards. He had planned the whole thing.

As far as I know, their relationship was better from that day onward. My brother's view of the batter got a much needed change.

Maybe something happened to us. We blamed God and keep ourselves from Him. We associate pain with Him. We fear we'll get hurt again. Recognize that many of the ways we think of God need to be changed – and overcome them.

Instead of running from Him, fall into the arms of the one who truly loves you…

… who always has… and always will.

Reading: Psalm 103

**"Altering your view of God,
will alter your life."**

Day 39

What the Easter Bunny Dragged In and Avoiding Robbery in the Pews

How's your commitment to your church?

"Spotty" is the most accurate answer for many Christians. It was never meant to be so casual. The connection with the body of Christ is meant to be one that's vital, dynamic, and strong.

"Hey, I can worship God anywhere. I don't have to be in church" lots of people say. And yeah, there's no better way to live than to worship God everywhere, moment by moment, with every breath.

But one of those places must be at church on a regular basis. By remaining separate from the body of Christ, you'll be out of step with the plan of God. Both for what you'll miss, and for what you'll take from others.

One reason is simply that God has chosen to make church a significant way that He changes, leads, and supports us. This is His chosen means. So, just worshipping Him anywhere without being at church is a take from you.

It's also God's plan that you be there because Church is not just what we get from it but what we contribute. If you're not involved, others miss out on your gifts and talents. They miss out on just your presence and fellowship. Not being there is a take from others.

No wonder God calls us to church commitment!

Internalize this:

> **And let us consider how we may spur one another on toward love and good deeds, not giving up meeting together, as some are in the habit of doing, but encouraging one another.**
>
> **Hebrews 10:24-25**

Mortified!

"Welcome. So glad you're here. Is this your first time with us?" I asked one man on his way out of the church on Easter.

With a look of complete disdain, he answered, "Pastor, how can you say that?! I've been coming to this church for years!"

"Oh no," I thought, "I've really blown it now." It was one of those terrible moments pastors have nightmares about. Here's a guy I've completely overlooked. Maybe he's someone whose name I've been told over and over and I still don't know it. Maybe he's in the choir and I've not even noticed him. Maybe he's on the Board!

I was embarrassed… but then he said it. "Yeah, Pastor, I'm here every Easter."

How do you think I felt then? Vindicated. Yes, perfectly vindicated. The redness in my face? Gone. Very much gone!

To him, coming once a year made him kind of a regular. It made him someone whom I should know. Many people have a similar idea of regular church attendance. Even if they attend only every month's fifth Sunday, they're "regulars" at church.

What are they missing? What are they taking from the others in the pews? The challenge here is to make your commitment to your church a real one that reflects a true conviction of the greatness church can have in your life and the greatness you can contribute to others by being there.

Be sure to get what God has for you. Be sure to give to others what God has to give them through you.

Avoid robbery in the pews.

Be there.

Reading: 1 Corinthians 12:12-27

**"Church is not just what we get from it but
what we contribute by being there."**

Day 40

A Straw Emergency and the Inner Person of the Heart

Back away from the mirrors!

Sometimes we can be very concerned about our appearance. That is, absolutely overly concerned with it often.

No wonder the Bible talks about how much it's what is inside that counts. It's what is inside that we should be giving so much of our attention.

In fact, to the Pharisees, Jesus said that the outward appearance of righteousness is all that mattered to them. The inside of the "cup" was dirty. From Proverbs we see, "Beauty is fleeting and charm is deceitful but a woman who fears [meaning believes in and follows] the Lord is to be praised".

When we put our emphasis on what is outside, our priorities are way off from the Lord's and from where they need to be.

What a transformation happens when we take our hearts to task.

What a transformation when we clean the inside of the cup.

Internalize this:

> **Man looks at the outward appearance,
> but the Lord looks at the heart.**
>
> **1 Samuel 16:7**

Ever been on a date where you hope everything goes well but it doesn't? (Maybe you're saying this is every date you ever had.)

That happened to me in a big way once. We were having lunch when, oddly enough, my tongue got stuck in the straw, right in the middle of our meal.

You would think someone could negotiate a straw after years of drinking things, but not that day.

I wish I could say I'm just kidding with you but I'm not. The straw was harder than a usual straw. It developed cracks on both sides. My tongue got caught in the slits.

With all the things to get you at lunch – like knives, hot soups, a food allergy, something caught in your throat, I was nabbed by the straw.

There's no Heimlich for this!

As my date was talking, I interrupted with these words, "I'll be alright." Only I didn't say those words as clearly as they are written here. Try holding your tongue right now and saying it. That's how it came out.

What a great impression I must have been making! "Yes. We have a winner here." She must have sarcastically been thinking.

What if paramedics had to come? During the 'rescue' would we have heard those common phrases like "Don't panic! You'll be alright."? And, to onlookers, "Nothin' to see here!"? They don't have those "jaws of life" things for tongues and straws do they? I hope not.

I am so glad she looked at more than the surface appearance. I'm so glad she looked passed a guy with his tongue caught in a straw, mumbling things, wondering about paramedics. I did get another date with her!

Looking at your own heart and the hearts of others is what we all must do. Put far more emphasis on what is inside of you and others.

Know God looks at the heart.

Be a man or woman who believes and follows the Lord above all else.

This is to be praised.

Reading: Proverbs 31:10-31 and Matthew 23:25-28

**"Buy a car for its engine.
See people for their hearts."**

Day 41

Valuing the Words "See You in a Year" and Valuing Being With the Hurting

"Say what Doc?"

You've probably experienced this before: You get a cold, or eat some bad cashew chicken and end up sick and hurting. Often it's much more serious. Beyond the obvious, the worst part is how it seems like the whole world just keeps on running without us. The loneliness and isolation makes the illness far worse.

Hospital walls or bedroom walls can close in pretty fast. If you get a call from a friend when you're feeling like this, it's like they've done something profoundly moving by reaching out to you in your misery and isolation.

They don't even have to say much of anything. It's not so much their words – it's more the idea that they noticed you, that they missed you, that they cared enough to do something, and that the world hasn't completely forgotten you. "Being with" like this brings them a powerful connection back to the world.

It's the same for people who've had a loss ("small" or devastating), who are in prison, who are having any other kind of trouble. They need a visit, a call, a card, an email, a text, a Facebook message, a tweet. They need you in some way.

Making that connection is a lot easier than you might think – and it makes a bigger difference than you can ever imagine.

Internalize this:

> **Truly I tell you, whatever you did for one of the least of these brothers and sisters of mine, you did for me.**
>
> **Matthew 25:40**

When you go to the doctor there are things you want to hear and things you don't. Here's a few you want:

"You're a hypochondriac. Get out of here." That's right, you want the doctor shooing you out of his office since he has patients with real problems.

"I got a cream for that. It will just take two weeks." "Cream" and "two weeks" are usually really good things to hear.

"See you in a year." You want to hear the word "year" somewhere in regard to your next visit.

Some things you don't want to hear from your doctor:

"I don't know what that is. I'll have to ask around, read up some more. Have never seen that before." Yeah, just what you want, the doctor having to do additional research because of you.

"Hey, come see this!" Also undesirable – your doctor calling over colleagues to see this puzzling, baffling, unique thing going on with you. "Does your church have a prayer chain?" Yeah this is bad… and if the doctor asks about your church's meals for the shut-ins program for your sake, not good.

I once called up a church member who got one of those not-so-good news calls. I figured I would take him out to lunch to cheer him up. My call didn't start out that way, however. "Hey, Jack, this is Doug LaPointe calling. Can I take you to lunch?" Silence. And then a very anxious question, "Who? Dr. Lee?"

He thought his doctor was calling to take him to lunch. No wonder he was worried. Your doctor may be very good but they're not gonna call to take you to lunch.

In fact I have this theory. If your doctor does call you out of the blue to take you to lunch, you failed whatever test they gave you. If your doctor calls to take you to dinner, that's your personal last supper. He was really glad to find out it was me, not his doctor.

But, remember those around you on special occasions and when they are sick and hurting. Take advantage of all the opportunities to help others at those key times. Know what great a difference it makes.

Live by the principle that what you do to others, you do to the Lord.

"Be with".

Reading: Matthew 25:31-46

"Little acts of kindness are not so little."

Day 42

A One-Day Boxing Career
and Winning Spiritual Battles

One of the keys to winning any fight is assessing your opponent correctly.

Failure to account for their strengths and weakness could prove fatal for you. So, a prepared warrior never underestimates their opponent's strengths nor overestimates their weakness but knows them well.

You're in a battle.

And it's serious. It's with the devil. This battle's going to call on every ounce of "warrior" you can bring forth at times. Underestimating his strengths is deadly. His intent is to kill, maim, and destroy you.

If you think the devil is just this cute little thing in a red suit, or that maybe he doesn't exist at all, you're underestimating him.

If you underestimate your opponent, you're unprepared for battle.

Likewise, failing to realize the devil's weakness, that is, that he is completely defeated in Christ and no temptation is too great for you, also leaves you unprepared for battle.

He has no power over you, except what you give him. He cannot even attempt anything except what God allows.

If you overestimate your opponent, you're unprepared for battle.

Internalize this:

> **Cast all your anxiety on him because he cares for you. Be self-controlled and alert. Your enemy the devil prowls around like a roaring lion looking for someone to devour. Resist him standing firm in your faith.**

> **1 Peter 5:7**

My boxing career was short-lived. Very short-lived.

One day, in fact.

When I was young, my father took me and my brothers to a boxing ring where you could try out boxing. I got all psyched up about it and decided to enter the ring with a guy who, though young like me, looked a little more comfortable there. You know, he looked like he had been there before, in fact, often. He had.

As we sparred, at first I thought he was just a terrible boxer. He didn't punch. He didn't move fast. Nothing like that at all. I thought I could take him easily. I gave him a few punches. He didn't fall or anything but I was clearly winning… that is, if we actually had judges or something.

Then, one punch from him. That's all it took. I knew right then and there this guy had merely been toying with me and I had no business in this ring with him.

Because I underestimated him, I lost. If he would have overestimated me, thought I was much more than I was, perhaps he would've lost. He didn't though. No, he didn't overestimate me at all, I don't think. My boxing career was over.

Do not underestimate the devil. He is real. You will get attacked.

Be ready in the full armor of God. Resist him standing firm in the faith. Be alert and in prayer. Be strong in the Lord and in his mighty power.

Do not overestimate him, either. Know that in Christ, he has truly lost.

Know in faith you will extinguish all the flaming arrows of the evil one.

Assess correctly and win in the Lord!

Reading: Ephesians 6:10-18

"We are vulnerable to the devil when we over or underestimate him."

Day 43

Hot Dog Eating Contests
and Winning at What Really Counts

"How much for that?"

Some things in life are more worthwhile then others. We are constantly assessing the value of what we do and don't do and then follow through based on the value we have given it.

The most important things to us naturally are given the greatest effort and energy. And, by definition, whatever is our highest priority, we sacrifice everything else for.

This then is the key to spiritual growth. Our relationship with Christ must be held above everything else. It must be seen as being of much more value than anything.

There is not really a secret as to how to grow in Christ. No, it is the same as everything else in life. If we hold growth as the most worthwhile thing, if it is given the spot of highest priority, we will give it our greatest effort and energy.

Jesus said it's like a man who found a treasure in a field. Upon finding the treasure, he sells all to buy the field. He responded to the treasure as his highest priority and so nothing got in the way of getting it. He sold all for it.

We have found that treasure in Christ.

We must live like it is our treasure and grow.

Internalize this:

> **Jesus replied: 'Love the Lord your God with all your heart and with all your soul and with all your mind.' This is the first and greatest commandment.**
>
> **Matthew 22:37-40**

"You didn't just eat 60?!"

Every now and then you hear of one of those hot dog eating contests. First of all, I don't know how they do it. I mean if I'm hungry I can eat one maybe two hot dogs. Not sure but I doubt I have ever eaten three. I wish it weren't so, but the winner each year of hot dog contests is eating like 50 or 60 of these things.

But more than that, I don't know why they do it. In fact, I have just one question about the person who eats the most… are they really the winner?

I don't think so.

Now I have to ask. Is this something you should put on your resume or be certain to leave off? Usually you want to put down things you have won and all your accomplishments. But you put down that you ate 60 hot dogs and I'm not sure you're going to get that corner office job.

If you do get the job, I don't think you're getting invited to the company picnic. "Yeah we think it would be better that you take that day off instead. We have only ordered 40 hot dogs for the whole office."

Contests like this hot dog eating one, can remind us that we put a lot of effort into some things that aren't worth it. I'm sure you can think of things in your life and past that fit that category. Then, we can put little effort into things that are well worth all that we have.

Growing in Christ is one of those things some people put little effort into. But it is the treasure we have found. Make growing in Him your highest priority giving Him all that you are.

Let those things not so worth it go down in priority in your life. Ask God to help you identify what you have given too much priority to. He will show you! Know these are the things in the way of giving growth in Christ your highest priority. Instead, love the Lord with all your heart, soul, and mind.

Get the treasure!

Reading: Matthew 13:36-46

"Your highest priority gets your most attention."

Day 44

A Few Wrong Numbers
and the Problem of Being Too Busy

Somebody once said, "If you're too busy for God, you're too busy."

So true! Yet we seem to get so busy and running around too fast all the time. Next thing you know, God and doing the things that would please Him are crowded out.

Some have called this the "tyranny of the urgent". The immediate things in front of us seem so important at the time, it's all we ever really get to. So, these things tyrannize us. Sometimes we need to make a concerted effort to get to what really matters in our life, and stop being "tyrannized by the urgent".
.

Often we look at being busy or dealing with the urgent with a sense of pride. The busier we are with things like this, the more efficient at life we must be. Perhaps we think we are more important. Maybe others think we are successful since we are so busy – and we buy into that.

All that may really be happening is that we're just tyrannized by the urgent.

We need to get back to what really matters.

Internalize this:

> **The plans of the diligent lead to profit as surely as haste leads to poverty.**

> **Proverbs 21:5**

363-8009. Sounds like an innocent enough phone number, right?

It was mine, and I'm here to tell you it was not so innocent. I had it as an associate pastor – my direct line.

The problem?

It was one digit off from a very popular pizza place down the street called Knock Out Pizza. The number at the pizza place was 364-8009.

"Yeah, I'd like two pepperoni pizzas, large – delivered." This is what I heard of the person who misdialed by one in their haste.

Now, I could be nice and just give the caller the correct phone number. But there was a time or two when I wasn't in a good mood, and I was tempted to just take the order. "What's that? You want two large pepperoni pizzas? That's great. It will be ready in ten minutes."

It got worse. There was a veterinarian's office in the area that had 363-0809. Imagine what this call may have been like if I thought they were talking about a kid in youth group not their dog.

Caller: "Um, Max is biting again… do you think we should put him down?"
Me: "NO, NO, don't even say that!"
Caller: "How about we give him away?"
Me: "NO, NO not that either! You must deal with your frustration better!"
Caller: "Well, I think we should at least put him in the garage until he stops."
Me: "I'm calling the police!"

This is some of what happens when we are just in too much of a hurry! Now a couple wrong numbers as a result of being in a hurry may not be too much to worry about, but often the consequences are much worse.

Know how important it may be to slow down, live for more than the immediate urgent things, and get to what's really important.

Know that haste can lead to many problems.

Dial the right phone numbers… and dial the right priorities too.

Keep the things God calls you to above all.

Reading: Luke 10:38-42

"If we are too busy for God, we are too busy."

Day 45

Digging for Treasure in Your Backyard
and Digging for Treasure From God

Your life is the sum of the choices you've made.

The right decisions in life can hardly be overestimated. We live and die by the choices we make. The wisdom we show not only establishes our life but affects others too. Decision-making doesn't occur in a vacuum. Wise choices go out and touch other's lives even generations later. Wisdom is far reaching and mighty in impact.

Proverbs says, "Take my instruction and not silver, and knowledge rather than choicest gold. For wisdom is better than jewels; and all desirable things cannot compare with her."

Foolishness is real similar, only in the opposite direction. Foolishness affects our life and almost always extends to affect others too. It can affect the lives of people we have never met, thousands of them, generations later. Like wisdom, foolishness has a long arm.

So, of the foolish, God warns, "Ruin and misery mark their ways, and the way of peace they do not know." Ultimately, life can be real forgiving of the little things we do wrong. But, it's not so forgiving of the big mistakes that show we lacked wisdom. Those can stay with us. The Bible calls us to diligently seek wisdom and make the right choices as if our life and the lives of others depend on it.

They do.

Internalize this:

> **If you call out for insight and cry aloud for understanding, and if you look for it as for silver and search for it as for hidden treasure, then you will understand the fear of the Lord and find the knowledge of God.**

> **Proverbs 2:3-5**

There are some really good things about being a kid.

As a kid, you get driven wherever you need to go. The only adults who have drivers are celebrities and the very wealthy. As a kid, you never fight for the check at a restaurant. Nope. Someone a little bigger than you always pays it. Sweet.

And, I wish some of the things we believed as kids could be true. I remember one thing many of us in our neighborhood believed was that if you just dug a little in our backyard, you could find buried treasure just about anywhere.

That's right. We sort of had this picture of the world that went like this. There is grass. Under the grass, there is dirt. About four feet below that layer, treasure. All over the world, just like that.

Now we weren't picky about what kind of treasure we would dig up. It could be actually gold and jewels. It could also be just some priceless artifacts or stuff museums longed to have. Any of these types of treasure would be fine. So, we dug a lot. Whole areas of our yard were dedicated to digging.

We had an aunt and uncle who once snuck out at night and put coins in the holes we dug to further the myth… with my parent's full knowledge and approval. What deceitful people!

But, it all came to an abrupt end too. My parents put in a pool.

Eventually we grew up and realized the only thing under dirt is more dirt. Sometimes some trash or an old tire. Ah, welcome to adulthood. But according to Scripture, this is a childhood belief that can, in a way, come true. The Bible says that if we dig for wisdom from God, we will always find. It is right there below the surface everywhere we dig.

Dig for it! Get wisdom from God. Never stop digging. Search for it as for hidden treasure.

Know you will always find.

Reading: Proverbs 2

"Wisdom is buried treasure waiting to be found."

Day 46

Pulling a Boat with Your Teeth and Fulfilling Your Call to Ministry

Sometimes I think we can spend a little too much time criticizing others.

Part of the reason is as one person once said, "We judge ourselves by our intentions but others by their actions." Uh-oh. That's a problem. That's one standard for us, and another for the rest of the world.

Another problem with the critic is they often feel they are accomplishing so much more than they really are. After all, criticizing makes people feel so much superior. With all this superiority they are doing a lot of good, right? Wrong.

Someone once pointed out that there has never been a monument made to a critic. They aren't the ones accomplishing all that much.

What is more, critics tend to be the least able to receive any criticism of themselves. It's been said, "Constructive criticism is when I criticize you. Destructive criticism is when you criticize me."

Benjamin Franklin once said, "Any fool can criticize, condemn, and complain, and most fools do."

People with their sleeves rolled up doing ministry don't have time or energy to be so critical of everyone else. They are busy. They are also making their own errors and can deal with others in an understanding way rather than just as a critic. In fact, I think it's true that it is when you do nothing you start feeling like the expert. If you're doing nothing, you're making no errors.

Don't get me wrong. There is an important place for critiquing others in this world. But, for some, it has simply taken over who they are. It is too much of all they do.

For many of us, doing a lot more in ministry and criticizing a lot less, is God's call.

Internalize this:

'Come, follow me,' Jesus said, 'and I will make you fishers of men.' At once they left their nets and followed him.

Matthew 4:19-20

The guy was lifting a bus!

Ever watch those Strongman competitions? You know, the ones where these incredibly strong men are doing unbelievable feats of strength.

They are tugging boats and buses. They are lifting families and pulling out trees and whatever else someone can dream up.

One of the things I like is that no one can Monday-morning quarterback them. I mean, you can't look at a guy who is pulling a boat with his teeth and be like, "No, no, no. That's not the way I do that. You have to get it in the back of the mouth or the boat will never go."

Or to that guy about to lift a bus, "When you lift that bus, try getting a good grip on the tailpipe. That's what I do." No. But, I have noticed people will Monday-morning quarterback over just about anything else while doing very little themselves.

Determine not to just be a spectator or critic. There is no spiritual gift of critic ever mentioned in the Bible.

Use the gifts God has given you and put away a critical heart. Know how much your gifts will bless others and how little your critiques of them may be doing.

Be engaged in deep significant ministry.

Leave the role of critic and spectator behind when it has come to dominate your life.

Reading: Matthew 28:1-20

"There is no such thing as a spiritual gift of critic."

Day 47

Learning to Drive the Hard Way
and Living Full Out for Christ

Want to grow in Christ?
Really?

You can probably sense God calling you in, deeper and more intimate with Him.

And while this may be your greatest desire, it is also likely that you've got competing commitments. These are things standing in the way of all the growth God desires for you.

You move forward by your commitment to Christ but not as much as you could, because your competing commitments hold you back.

A competing commitment can be some way of living you refuse to let go of. It can be a habit you choose to keep. It can be false beliefs you cling to about yourself, God, or others. It could be worry, or a lack of forgiveness toward others.

All of these things compete against your desire for growth and fruitfulness in Christ and accomplishing everything God has for you. As Christ said, "A house divided against itself cannot stand."

Competing commitments like that need to go from our lives.

Growth needs to happen unhindered.

Internalize this:

> **For the wages of sin is death, but the gift of God is eternal life in Christ Jesus our Lord.**
>
> **Romans 6:23**

Get off the sidewalk!

I remember when I first started driving. I don't think I will ever forget it… and anyone unlucky enough to share the road with me back then isn't likely to forget it either.

There's a good reason insurance companies charge so much more to ensure new drivers. In my case, the jacked-up premium probably came from my practice of driving with both feet – one for the gas and one for the brake. Crazy, right?

It's very likely that a driver like that is going to press the gas and brake at the same time. Good drivers drive with one foot for the brake and gas, either stopping or going – but not both at the same time.

I'm not sure exactly what happens if you press the brake and gas at the same time or one just before the other. And, I don't really want to find out. I suppose you may spin out, stop altogether, or kill a nearby squirrel.

Maybe this is why teens do donuts in parking lots a lot – feet on both pedals. Whatever it is that does happen, it's not good. It's not how it's meant to be. And all the while driving exams test whether or not we can parallel park. They've got bigger things to think about out there than that!

Now here's the thing. You're likely doing the very same thing in your life and walk with God. We have a foot on the gas and one on the brake. We want to grow but we also hold on to competing commitments.

We're meant to press the gas and go! We're meant to grow stronger in our faith, finding and fulfilling our purpose in Christ.

The challenge to you today is to choose to take your foot off the brake, and keep it on the gas, driving deeper and further into your relationship with God.

Discover and get rid of those competing commitments!

Speed forward in growth.

Reading: Romans 6:15-23

"A heart divided goes in circles."

Day 48

A Stand In For Me at My Relatives and Receiving the Grace of God

Salvation is by grace.

We may have heard that many times. But what does it mean?

It means someone did something for you that you could never do. More specifically, it means Christ died for you, in your place, the death you deserved but could not pay. He paid it.

Jesus Christ is God, the second person of the Trinity. He became a man by the virgin birth. He was fully God and fully man. God dwelt among us. He died for us.

He could pay the penalty for our sin since He had no penalty to pay for His own. Paul reports, "He is the atoning sacrifice for our sins."

Our good works amount to nothing. We are in complete reliance on Christ for getting forgiveness.

So He calls us to Himself asking only that we receive Him, receive what He has done for us. Walk in grace. Without the grace, there would be no way of getting right with God. But, "Believe on the Lord Jesus and you will be saved."

By His grace, everyone who calls on Him is placed in right standing with God now and forever.

By His grace we have forgiveness and eternal life.

Internalize this:

> **For all have sinned and fall short of the glory of God, and all are justified freely by his grace through the redemption that came by Christ Jesus.**
>
> **Romans 3:23-24**

Too many Christmas cards!

Ever notice how at Christmas time, there are more and more opportunities for people to do things for you? You could probably always get people to gift-wrap for you or bake for you. That's good.

But now there are people who will put up and take down Christmas decorations for you. In fact, it's not even your own decorations that they put up but theirs – their tree, their ornaments, their blinking lights, their reindeer on your front lawn. All put up, taken down, and supplied by someone else. Just call them.

There are also people now who will write your Christmas cards for you. Give them a list and you're done. They will even check the list twice, put the postage on, and drop them in a mailbox. Seriously. I know. Some of you are out there saying, "Get me their number!"

I wonder what's next. Will there be people to go and visit your relatives at Christmas for you? Your relatives just see this unknown guy at their house. He eats the dinner. He gives compliments. He opens your gifts and says, "That's perfect. How did you know?"

Then there is always that one relative who will say to your fill-in, "You haven't changed a bit!" as she pinches them on the cheek.

You're home getting things done.

Maybe all of this, people-doing-things-for-you thing, is actually very appropriate as part of the celebration of Christmas… a symbol of how we could never have been saved on our own. Jesus Christ had to be born and die for us.

Celebrate His grace, His unmerited favor, in your life. Know salvation is not by works or anything we could do.

Know it is through Christ, the God-man, the sinless one, who died in your place, doing it all for you.

Walk in His grace!

Reading: Isaiah 9:2-7

"Grace really is amazing."

Day 49

Egg Man on the Corner
and the Importance of Thinking Ahead

Some people are already saving for their kid's college or their own retirement right when they start working. Some teenagers are already praying for their future husband or wife, someone they may not meet for years to come.

Others… not so much.

They kind of live life by the seat of their pants. They make choices on a whim according to how they feel in the moment. Usually choices like this really cost us. They come with a price, a consequence we didn't see. We make the rash choice. We pay the price later.

God calls us to be the kind of decision maker who plans ahead and goes on to choose very wise things.

We see Joseph led all of Egypt to think years ahead and prepare by storing food for a severe famine. It saved them.

You can go either way with your choices. But one leads to destruction, the other to reward.

Impulse purchases and impulse decisions often end up the same way.

In regret.

Internalize this:

Therefore be as shrewd as snakes and as innocent as doves.

Matthew 10:16

"Who's Donna?"

You know how you see guys on the side of the road dressed as something strange to get you to come in and buy what the store is selling? There is a guy dressed as a chicken outside of a fried chicken place. Maybe a guy dressed as a pizza or even a pancake.

There's even a guy near where I live who dresses as an egg. Now I think the egg is about as low on the food chain as you can get. In fact, I think the chicken guy, the pizza guy, and the pancake make fun of the egg guy.

The worst part about this is that I don't think there is even a breakfast place where this guy hangs! It's just his outfit for the day. Even if there were a place he was advertising, I don't think I could eat eggs from a guy like this. "Hey, come over here. Let me cook you some eggs." No, that's not gonna work.

Now, the other day I saw a guy with a tattoo sign with a big arrow pointing to a tattoo shop. Now, I have nothing against many people's tattoos, but don't you have to think ahead about a thing like that?

I mean, I can understand seeing a chicken guy and realizing you haven't had lunch and getting to that chicken place. But, I can't see looking at a sign for a tattoo and quickly getting over a couple of lanes, veering off the road to suddenly get to that tattoo shop saying something like, "Oh yeah. I almost forgot! I gotta get a tattoo!"

You shouldn't be saying to all the cars you just cut off, "Suddenly realized I needed a tattoo. I'm sure you understand." I mean, these things are usually permanent, right? People have tattoos of girlfriend's names they broke up with 20 years ago, right? "Donna and Mike Forever". Who's Donna?

No, you think these things out. You take your time. In fact, go get some chicken, pizza, pancakes, or eggs and think about things.

Avoid being rash about any choice that matters. Plan ahead. Know the consequences of your choices. Take advantage of the fact that forethought usually pays off.

Be shrewd as a snake and innocent as a dove.

Reading: Genesis 25:27-34 and 41:46-57

**"Life is designed to reward forethought
and punish impulsiveness."**

Day 50

A Rookie Mom's Mistake
and How to Share the Gospel

Many people celebrate Easter. Not as many know what it's really about.

The basic message of the gospel is not a complicated one. It's a four-fold message and it goes like this:

God loves you and wants to have a personal relationship with you.

We are sinful and have chosen to reject God. We have become separated from Him and guilty before Him.

God sent his Son, Jesus Christ, to die on the cross for our sin so that we could know God and be restored to Him.

We must receive Christ into our lives repenting of our sin. When we do, we become forgiven and right with God for all eternity.

By the death of Christ, He conquered sin and death for us. This was demonstrated in His rising again leaving the empty tomb. Now we can be forgiven of our sin and come to know God personally.

There could be no two greater needs met than these two.

That's Easter.

Internalize this:

> **For there is one God and one mediator between God and men, the man Christ Jesus.**
>
> **2 Timothy 2:5**

Rookie!

It was a mom's first year to hide the Easter eggs for all the kids in her mom's group. How exciting! The kids always loved the Easter egg hunt every year. What could go wrong?

Well, rookies do make mistakes. This mom did too. She hid the eggs well enough. And, you know, there is a skill to that too. If you hide them too easily, the hunt goes too fast and the kids feel gypped.

Hide them where it is too hard to find and that's when you start finding the eggs when you least expect to… like at the Fourth of July picnic. You also need to count to make sure all the eggs were retrieved. If you wonder why, see previous result.

Well, this rookie mom passed all those little tests. Her mistake? She didn't fill the eggs with anything. You know how it's supposed to go. The kids find the eggs. But the point of finding the eggs is to get the candy that was placed inside. There was no candy inside these.

The kids ran to find those eggs. They looked hard. They fought when there was a tie. Yes, all those things. But all for no candy. Oh the looks of disappointment! Oh the humanity! What a sham!

Not to worry. Those kids will get over it… you know, after a few years with good therapy and support groups. Well, it's one thing to miss the point of an Easter egg hunt. That's really no big deal. But it's another to miss the point of Easter.

Know the four points of the gospel. Know why the tomb was empty and why it matters – Christ defeated sin and death for us. Respond to these four points and share them!

Know there is nothing more significant than what Christ's death and resurrection brings to us!

Forgiveness and new life!

Reading: 1 Corinthians 15:1-22

"The gospel is simple in content, profound in influence."

Day 51

A Homecoming for a Golf Team and Great Reward in Heaven

"Well done!"

Someday, all you do for the kingdom of God will be celebrated and rewarded. How amazing! How wonderful! That's someday, however – not now.

In fact, right now, rather than recognition, you can expect persecution for the things you do for the Kingdom. How important it is to realize that the world will oppose what you do – and to be ready for that response.

As Christians, we're operating in a different economy. Notice how Christ was rejected, even after doing many miracles in their midst, speaking the truth, and dying for them.

The world throws away the things that matter most.

A servant is not above his master. We too will be treated this way since Christ was. You never want to look for – or need – recognition from a world that denies God. Their response should never dictate your life and service.

Someday you will get a very different response.

That's the one that matters!

Internalize this:

> **And when the Chief Shepherd appears,
> you will receive the crown of glory that will never fade away.**
>
> **1 Peter 5:4**

No cheerleaders. No pep rally. Nothing.

I played golf in high school. The problem with playing golf in high school is you don't have all the fans that other sports get.

You never hear people yelling, "Make that putt! Make that putt!" from the sidelines. There's no Homecoming match where the school's having bonfires and dances for golfers. Nope. None of that.

Maybe we should've tried putting that black stuff under our eyes and crashing our heads together. No. There just wasn't going to be anyone cheering us on.

That, in part, is why I loved what the golf coach did at the end of one season. He threw a big BBQ at his house: burgers, chicken, ribs, corn, cake, ice cream… he had it all there for us. Yum.

He went even further and had made awards for us, too. There was "Putter of the Year". The coach had actually added up all of our putts in every match and knew who took the least putts. He had many other awards too. "Wow", I thought.

I've thought about that BBQ a lot over the years because it's a picture, I think, of heaven. Right now the world rejects or just ignores us and what is done for God. But there will be a day when all is revealed and the things we have done for the Kingdom celebrated.

Don't look for or need recognition from the world. Anxiously look for that day when the response to what you do is the appropriate response. The response the Lord gives.

Know He will give us crowns to lay down at His feet. Reward that never fades away!

Let this spur you on to all God calls you to do…

… and help you stand firm when you don't get that response now.

Reading: Matthew 5:1-12

"We may not be told what our influence for Christ is now but we need to know it now."

Day 52

Running Out of Candy
and How God Provides

How much do you trust God?

Do you worry? Do you envy and covet feeling there is a great lack?

Hey, we all fall short in these areas – and we know it. We read it all over the place in the Bible how we are to trust and not worry… but fall short.

God provides for birds. God provides for plants and grass. So what, is He going to leave us hanging? No way! Not in the area of your relationships, your career, your finances, your health – not at all. After, all, He lacks nothing, always has an abundance.

God takes excellent care of His children. Because of His promises in this, we're called not to worry or envy or covet. Actually, we're warned about these things and how destructive they are, how they lead to other destructive things.

The more we will trust God, the better off we will be.

And this is the lifestyle God has called for.

Internalize this:

> **But seek first his kingdom and his righteousness, and all these things will be given to you as well.**
>
> **Matthew 6:33**

Trick or Treat!

Ever start running out of candy on Halloween night?

I could feel this start happening to me one year. I gave out too much early on. My son tried to warn me, "Dad, don't do that!", but I didn't listen.

I started rationing but this got rather awkward. I mean you can't give one candy corn, can you? You can't give a pack a gum to five kids and say, "Split it."

I began thinking of alternatives to give out, but I definitely didn't want to be nickel guy or penny lady. We hated that when we were kids! So back to possible food solutions. But didn't want to be baggie of Cheerios guy either. I once was at the door of a guy who got the knock on Halloween and scrambled around to come up with a Granola bar ten minutes later. Didn't want to be that guy.

Desperate, all I could think of saying was, "Here is a stick of butter and some sugar. Make your own." I even almost moved to household items, "Here how 'bout this lamp? Just take it, I'm out of candy." "Here's a green shirt for you… goes well with the Frankenstein mask."

I was out. I had to turn out the porch light and everyone thereafter had to pass by my house.

Many think of God a bit like this though. They think maybe He just doesn't have enough. Maybe He's rationing or just barely able to give to me or anyone. Maybe He's baggie of Cheerios guy, Granola boy, or penny lady!

Then worry, envy, and anger.

No way!

Know God always has and so we are to always ask and always know He will provide all the wisdom, help, guidance, and everything else we need.

Trust and do not worry or do anything that demonstrates you think He cannot provide.

Seek Him first and know that with God…

… the porch light is always on.

Reading: Matthew 6:25-34 and 7:7-11

"With God, the porch light is always on."

Day 53

Swimming with Alligators
and Being a Leader in Christ

Ever get the feeling you're leading, but nobody's following?

As a genuine believer, you're most definitely in the minority. You are leading by following Christ with only a small percentage following. Jesus said, "But small is the gate and narrow the road that leads to life, and only a few find it."

And centuries earlier, God inspired Solomon to say basically the same thing: "I found one upright man among a thousand."

To be a leader, it is so important not to check what everyone else in the world is doing when it comes to following God. This is no time to let your life be run by opinion polls telling you what to do!

We're called to live lives very distinct from the ways of the world. Since the world does not know Him, they have a completely different set of priorities than a person who loves God above all.

If we love God, our lives ought to look very different from many around us. We ought to be like aliens and strangers in this world.

Being distinct from the world will be critical when it comes to following God and leading.

You will need to be like one in a thousand on the narrow road.

Internalize this:

> **Enter through the narrow gate. For wide is the gate and broad is the road that leads to destruction, and many enter through it. But small is the gate and narrow the road that leads to life, and only a few find it.**
>
> **Matthew 7:13-14**

I'm not going in there!

In Florida where I once lived, there are signs up all over the place that say, "Don't Molest the Alligators." Do we really have to be told not to mess around with things that could kill and eat us? What in the world are we in Florida thinking? Does this make any sense?

Do people in Maine have to be told not to mess with the giant black bears? Do they like have to be told not to stick their head in the bear's mouth or steal its food or call it names? No, they just post a sign with the picture of a bear. Enough said.

Do people from California have to be told, "Don't molest the mountain lions"? No, they run when they see them. But apparently people are messing with alligators just for fun and getting killed sometimes.

Recently I actually saw a sign that said, "Warning – Alligators" and beneath it, another that read, "No Swimming". I didn't think we should need the "Do not Molest" sign. But I really don't think we need these two signs together!

People must be out there saying, "Hey there might be alligators in there, Ed. Let's go for a swim anyway. Last one in is a rotten egg!" Which was actually probably the alligator's last meal before it got these two fresh swimmers.

They say common sense is not so common as these signs seem to indicate. But neither is following God.

Don't follow the beaten path. Stay a leader by following God. Don't look to see what others are doing with God to determine whether you will follow Him.

Be a follower of God and let your life be very different, an alien and stranger... a leader.

Be the one in a thousand.

Be on the narrow road.

Reading: 1 John 1:1-2:11

"If only one in a thousand is following the Lord, be the one."

Day 54

"Click It or Ticket"
and Seeing Your Significance

Significant to a lot of people!

When we come to Christ, suddenly we have a whole new mission in life. We are called to lead others to the lifesaving knowledge of Christ, the very thing they need most. Now that's important.

In fact, now that God can use us, we will be having 'divine appointments' all of our lives. God will be placing people into our lives that we will truly have a great impact upon.

It will be exciting as we see ourselves growing in our gifts and calling, as we see our lives have greater and greater impact on others. Untold numbers of people we have never met are actually counting on us and our faithfulness in ministry.

Now this is great purpose but it is not an overstatement in the least. Moses said our influence may be to a "thousand generations" because affecting one person usually means you have just affected many more.

One ripple in the water from a thrown stone leads to many ripples.

We don't just have impact.

We can leave a legacy!

Internalize this:

> **Those who cleanse themselves from the latter will be instruments for special purposes, made holy, useful to the Master and prepared to do any good work.**

> **2 Timothy 2:21**

I remember, shortly after I became a believer, reaching for my seatbelt in the car. Now, I always used my seatbelt before I became a believer. But I remember that now I was putting it on a little differently.

Now I put it on knowing that my life could have a huge impact on others. I knew the way to eternal life. I was living it. Others need what I have, the saving knowledge of Jesus Christ.

So, for the first time, I put that seat belt on as if the lives of others depend on it. I was not going to let all those lives that await me down. I saw a sign that was similar the other day. It told people as they left the parking lot to "Fasten seat belts. Someone needs you." How interesting I thought. That is the same sentiment I have had since I became a Christian.

On the other hand, I have also seen signs from law enforcement reading "Click It or Ticket". I am glad they are enforcing seat belt use but I can't help but think of the contrast here. How amazing to me that one's only motivation to wear their seatbelt would be they might get a ticket and not on the impact they could have on others.

Government can do a lot of things, but it shouldn't have to know the value of our lives more than we do. There should not be laws in place that show we do not appreciate fully just how much impact we can make on others.

Live all of your life now, as a believer, knowing of all the people who need you and will be blessed by you if you are faithful to God. Every time you put on your seatbelt, make it a memory trigger that you are greatly needed. Put you seatbelt on a little differently here on out thinking of all the people who are counting on you.

Take good care of yourself in every other way too knowing you have great purpose in life. Like when you are in a plane and they tell you to put your oxygen mask on first in an emergency before your children. Take care of yourself so you can help others.

Know the ripple and believe about the "thousand generations".

Create your legacy!

Reading: Matthew 13:1-23

"Put your oxygen mask on first."

Day 55

A Serbian Bishop in WW2 and the Importance of Forgiving Others

"Easier said than done!"

There are definitely some things that fit the category of easier said than done. Loving others is one of those things. "Love others." That was very easy to say (well, write). It is not as easy to always do.

Here's another. Forgive everyone who wrongs you. Interestingly, that was easy to write too. Much harder to do. When we are wronged, sometimes the last thing we want to do is forgive. Many of us hold grudges for a long time. Years. Decades. Lifetimes.

Yet, we are called to forgive no matter how hard that may seem to be too. Holding grudges makes no sense for the believer. After all, didn't Christ forgive us the great offense of our sin against him? Then how can we turn around and not forgive others for whatever relatively smaller offense they have committed against us?

As God is willing to forgive, so must we be. When all is said and done, the saying "To be forgiven is to be a forgiving person" is very true. And this is not to mention how harmful it is to hold a grudge. Bitterness will ruin us! We cannot let that happen. We need to forgive not for the sake of the person who wronged us, but for the effect it will have on us.

An unforgiving spirit is an emotional, social, and spiritual death-trap. It may even take a toll on us bodily! Solomon said, "A cheerful heart is good medicine, but a crushed spirit dries up the bones." Sure, forgiveness may be easier said than done but that doesn't mean it can be left undone.

It just means we need to make a greater effort to forgive.

Internalize this:

> **See to it that no one misses the grace of God and that no bitter root grows up to cause trouble and defile many.**

Hebrews 12:15

Often, great stories come out of atrocities when people rise to the occasion to love and forgive. Here is one such case. A Serbian Bishop, Nikolai Velimirovic, spoke out against Nazism in the early 1940s. Because of his protests, he was arrested and taken to the Dachau concentration camp.

The following was a prayer he wrote: "Bless my enemies, O Lord. Even [may] I bless them and do not curse them." His prayer goes on telling us how we can do this. "Enemies have driven me into your embrace more than friends have. Friends have bound me to Earth; enemies have loosed me from Earth and have demolished all my aspirations in the world." So we can bless our enemies since they have unwittingly blessed us with a better focus on the afterlife.

"Just as a hunted animal finds safer shelter than an un-hunted animal does, so have I, persecuted by enemies, found the safest sanctuary, having ensconced myself beneath your tabernacle, where neither friends nor enemies can slay my soul." We can bless our enemies since they have driven us to find safer shelter, the shelter the Lord provides. This is a shelter where you are truly safe.

In the same way, turn the tables on your initial thoughts about your enemies and see what good they have actually brought to you.

In this way, release them. Let them go from your heart's hold on them. Know how much better this will be for you. Know how it is needed to be a consistent person who has received God's forgiveness. Let no root of bitterness grow up and cause trouble.

Forgiving is easier said than done… but be sure to get it done.

Reading: Matthew 18:21-35

"**Forgive others. Not for their sake,**
but for yours."

Day 56

Indecisiveness at a Restaurant and Decisiveness about Eternal Life

The Bible tells us that we can be absolutely sure of where we will spend our eternity. In fact, it urges us to know.

If we have made the decision to receive Christ and He has come into our life, we know we have eternal life. There need not be any doubt in our minds. Here are a few ways we can know Christ is in our life:

We have new life in Him, life differently, and can tell God is present with us. Paul said, "He who is in Christ is a new creature, the old has passed away. All things have become new." The Holy Spirit Himself confirms to us that we have eternal life. The Bible says, "The Spirit himself testifies with our spirit that we are God's children. Now if we are children, then we are heirs [of heaven]." The Bible can also be affirmed as accurate by many objective tests. And the Bible reveals that if we have received Christ, we have eternal life.

It makes sense that God would not leave us doubting on this most essential thing, knowing where we will spend eternity. He hasn't. He causes us to know with certainty.

You can see that all the great believers in the Bible knew of their eternal life. It was not something they were unsure of. Paul, for example, said, "To live is Christ, and to die is gain." Many say they will find out when they die what happens to them. But it's too late once we die. Our eternity is set.

We must know now that it will be in heaven.

Internalize this:

> **I write these things to you who believe in the name of the Son of God so that you may know that you have eternal life.**

> **1 John 5:13**

Just five more minutes!

People choose at restaurants with varying levels of certainty. Have you ever noticed that? There is the person who knows exactly what they want. Sometimes they don't even need a menu. Waitress comes over and the decision is made.

For others it's a little bit of an ordeal. They not only need the menu, they read the whole thing. Waitress comes over and they say, "Give us a few more minutes." Waitress is thinking, "It's just lunch. It's sandwiches and soup. Maybe a half sandwich with a soup. Make a decision!"

Meanwhile, that type of guy asks everyone at their table what they are getting. If it were even remotely socially acceptable, they would probably ask the people at nearby tables too. When the waitress returns, that person has to go last to get a few more minutes of now rereading the menu in deep confusion and frustration… and slight panic.

Then, right after that person has made their order and the waitress walks away, they are the one who immediately says, "Oh, why did I order that!? What was I thinking!?" As soon as the food arrives, they are looking at everyone else's meal… with regret. All the others look better. They quickly ask everyone at the table if they can try theirs. They go halfsies with their spouse.

I think the buffet was invented for guys like that and their exasperated waitresses and dinner companions… "Let's just put everything out!" I think the drive-thru was invented for them too. Waitress is like, "Just pull around back and stay in your car. I will bring food to you."

You can be unsure of a lot of things in life like this, and that's okay. So, you get a bad meal or something, make people wait, frustrate a waitress. But if you aren't sure you have eternal life, this is something to make sure about. You should know Christ is in your life with certainty. If you are not sure, make certain. You need to know.

Be like the great saints of the Bible who all knew! Accept Christ into your life if you haven't.

And know you have.

Reading: John 1:1-18

"You can be unsure of a lot of things, but where you will spend eternity is something you must be sure about."

Day 57

High Schoolers Giving Autographs and Being a Good Role Model

You're a role model.

That's right. You are one. Every person is a role model because others are looking at you and to some degree model their life after you. It may be your children, your friends, your co-workers, but you are rubbing off on others.

The question then to ask is not whether you're a role model but whether you're a good one. The Apostle Paul was such a good role model, he even told others to "be imitators of me". Our goal should be to be able to say the same.

We can say "be imitators of me" if we are truly seeking the Lord with our whole heart and He really is the center of our life. Instantly you become someone to look at and model after.

Being a good role model doesn't mean perfection. No one is perfect. It means you're fully committed to the Lord, however. The key to handling our flaws is to be honest about them and grow out of them over time.

Being a good role model is one of the greatest joys. To know that by the way you live your life, you are leading other people to a closer walk with God is the only way to live.

To move from role model to good role model is the greatest shift anyone could make.

Internalize this:

Be imitators of me, just as I also am of Christ.

1 Corinthians 11:1

They're 15 years old!

I'll never forget as a kid going to the high school football games when I was just little, about eight or so. The crowd was full and excited, the players were great, the uniforms were sharp, the stadium itself was impressive and seemed really big. Hey, I even loved the hot dogs at half-time… it was all good to me.

In fact, I remember being so impressed that when the games were over, I and a lot of other kids wanted one more thing… the autographs of those great players.

That's right. They weren't getting out of there until they signed my pad. I was eight but I was determined. I was getting an autograph or two. Oh and what if they gave me a piece of a uniform, a smelly shirt, a mouthpiece? All the better!

I look back on that now, and what I didn't see then, was that those players whose autographs I wanted were merely high schoolers at a rather small town high school. But, I was looking up to them. They seemed like pros to me!

They probably had no idea of how anyone looked up to them since they were so young. But, they were role models to the point of giving autographs. In the same way, you may not realize it, but people look to you as a role model and what you do really matters.

When they look, are they seeing what they need to see? By looking at you, can they know how following God is meant to be? Can they do it too if they just imitate you?

Follow Christ with all you are and it will be very influential.

Don't wait for perfection. Be honest about your faults. Seek their removal too.

Know you're a role model.

Be a good one.

Reading: Hebrews 11:1-12

"The question is not whether we are role models but whether we are good ones."

Day 58

Cleaning Up Your Garage
and Cleaning Up Your Thought Life

Did you know that much of the outcome of our lives actually begins with just the thoughts we allow ourselves to have?

The thoughts we think actually lead to how we feel about life and ourselves. These feelings then lead to what we choose to do and not do. Thoughts then are like the seeds to a garden. You get what you plant.

No wonder Jesus urges us in the Sermon on the Mount, to guard our thought life not simply our actions. So He says don't lust, don't have anger towards anyone, forgive easily. All things in the mind!

Paul said he takes every thought captive to make it obedient to Christ. He takes his thoughts captive to what is right because they lead to so much more… and he knows it.

Think of your brain sort of as a house. You wouldn't bring garbage to sit in your house. To let ungodly thoughts in is acting just like that, with something even more important than our house – our mind.

No, instead you fix up your house and fill it with only the best of things. You make it a good home.

The mind is to be the same.

Internalize this:

> **Finally, brothers and sisters, whatever is true, whatever is noble, whatever is right, whatever is pure, whatever is lovely, whatever is admirable – if anything is excellent or praiseworthy – think about such things.**
>
> **Philippians 4:8**

"Yard Sale Today!"

Prices at yard sales are almost always real good. I think one reason is that the person holding the yard sale can see what a clean garage they could have if all that stuff sells. Their garage was a mess before they pulled all that out and plopped a "Yard Sale" sign down the street.

The garage seems much bigger than they thought too and they love this new space. They have started imagining what they could do with that new garage – put in a work table and build things. There could be doll houses, rocking chairs, bird houses. They're gonna be hero-dad and hero-granddad! They know it.

"Wow" they start to think. "I can't let anything back in that garage. If it doesn't sell, it is only a few feet to the curb and garbage day is Monday." And that thought right there is one reason prices are so low at garage sales! No one wants their messy garage back! No one wants to give up all those new possibilities!

So, the customer who happens to pass by and pull his car over, has all the bargaining power. He knows you love your clean garage. He knows that trash day is Monday!

He might be a terrible negotiator, but not at a garage sale. He gets all he wants for pennies on the dollar going home a big winner. That customer may have overpaid for everything their entire life, but they are not overpaying at your garage sale. No, not at all.

Oh the power of a clean garage! In comes the doll houses, rocking chairs, and everything else good! Want a cleaned out mind with lots of new possibilities too? Just begin a shift that says no more garbage in! Only the good stuff!

Watch what new possibilities immerge there… a thought life of purity, holiness, and love… at thought life free of bitterness, doubt, despair, lust and other thoughts like that.

Take every thought captive. Know this will change how you feel, what you do, and the outcome of your life.

Plant the right seeds!

Reading: 1 Peter 2:1-12

"Thoughts lead to feelings, which lead to actions, which help create the outcome of our lives."

Day 59

Deciphering Bad Handwriting
and Understanding God's Word

Mark Twain once said that it is not the things he cannot understand in the Bible that trouble him, but the things he can understand.

It's true that the Bible has many hard-to-understand passages. It's also true that the bulk of what we need to know is incredibly clear – and hard to hear sometimes.

In so many instances, it's a matter of applying what we already know, not knowing more. Putting those things we may not have liked to hear into practice.

It's no wonder the Bible warns us against just knowing the Word and not applying it. The temptation to do just that will be there.

In fact, the book of James tells us not applying the Word is like looking at your face in the mirror and then immediately forgetting what you look like. So, one minute we read what to do, but the next minute, at the point of application, we have forgotten what to do.

Wisdom is found not in acquiring knowledge, as great as that is, but in the application of knowledge. In fact, wisdom might be defined as knowledge applied.

Knowledge is never meant to just stay in a storeroom, so to speak. It's meant to be brought out like meat in a freezer when it's time to plan dinner. So many leave the meat in the freezer. Dinner never works that way.

Knowledge needs application.

Internalize this:

> Therefore everyone who hears these words of mine and puts them into practice is like a wise man who built his house on the rock.

Matthew 7:24-25

Can you believe the bad handwriting of doctors?

Believe me I'm not one to talk… but I don't write prescriptions either. I mean, if I were writing prescriptions, I would be writing in all block letters or something and writing really slowly. Better yet, I would be typing them out.

These are prescriptions! They can't make a mistake. Why are these prescriptions being written with such a cavalier nature? Why the scribble? Why the squiggly line that actually is supposed to communicate something?

A prescription for acne cannot become a prescription for hemorrhoids just from bad handwriting. A prescription for sinuses cannot become a cream for athlete's foot. No, may this never happen! Maybe that's one reason why pharmacists need years of education. Much of the time is on handwriting deciphering. You can't graduate until you can decipher squiggly little lines.

I could understand it better if this were going on in other professions. "Yes, he is a professional baseball player and look at that awful handwriting." That I can feel more comfortable about.

This way when everybody sees bad handwriting, they would say, "Must be a baseball player." As it is, when your handwriting is bad, they ask if you're a doctor. How did this happen?

Well, somehow these prescriptions do get read and everyone seems to know what they are doing at least most of the time, and that's great. But it also helps me to be grateful for the clarity of God's Word. The basics are rivetingly clear and we know them just as Mark Twain said.

Know that so much is not little, squiggly lines in the Bible, but obvious… like the greatest commandments. Love God. Love others.

Let us apply what we know from the Word of God… even the things we might not like.

And be wise.

Reading: Romans 1:16-20

"Better to know one thing and apply it, than know a thousand things and apply none of it."

Day 60

Making Good Calls as an Umpire
And Making Good Calls about Life

Others will have their opinions.

About what you ask? Everything! And many will also be sure to let you know it. They will have an opinion about you, about God, and everything in-between too.

You would think that the more inaccurate their opinion, the less vocal they would be about it. But this is usually not the case. People can be very sure and very outspoken over things they have no idea what they are talking about.

The Bible tells us of people like that and says "They do not understand either what they are saying or the matters about which they make confident assertions." Wouldn't it be nice if the less a person knows on a subject, the less they would speak about it?

People believe things for many wrong reasons other than what is reasonable and justified. Often it's just what people around them believe, so they believe it. Maybe there is something they gain if that idea of theirs is true… so they believe it. Either way, it is not about what is actually true.

So we sure need to be careful that we are not simply going by what others say. Sure, we need to get feedback from others and get wise counsel. But in the end, what ultimately matters is not other people's opinions…

… but God's.

Internalize this:

> **Trust in the Lord with all your heart**
> **and lean not on your own understanding;**
> **in all your ways submit to him,**
> **and he will make your paths straight.**

Proverbs 3:5-6

Baseball umpires are an interesting bunch to me.

I'm not sure I would ever want to be one. I mean, when was the last time you went to a game and you had to be completely neutral the whole time? It's impossible. That is the point of the game. No one is neutral. That is what sport is. The minute you become neutral, it is no longer a sport to you. So I admire refs and umpires and everything they do.

Now I am not sure why they have to get all animated about it sometimes though. Why does an ump yell "Strike three!!!" Can't they just say it? Maybe even whisper it? "Strike three" in a very low voice would work just as well.

I think they yell "Strike three" because they are just so upset with having to be neutral all the time. They are taking it out in other ways. If they could yell for one team or another I assure you that "Strike three" would come out as a whisper.

Well, my favorite umpire story came from an autobiography of an umpire named Bob Pinelli. He was an ump during the days of the great Yankee teams and the many greats on those teams, like Babe Ruth.

One day, Pinelli tells us that he called the Babe out on strikes. Everyone in Yankee stadium started booing. Babe turned to Pinelli and said, "There's 40,000 people here who know that the last pitch was a ball, tomato head." Pinelli looked back at Ruth and said, "Maybe so, Babe, but mine is the only opinion that counts."

Don't trust the fickle world that does not necessarily know what they so boldly proclaim. Realize their reasons for believing it may not even be to find truth! If it differs from God in any way, go with God. He always knows.

And if you wonder what God's opinion is of you, see Day 4 for starters. And if you wonder about what He thinks of many other things, see Day 59.

Live, believe, and trust that His is the only opinion that counts.

Reading: Proverbs 3:13-26

"God's opinion is the only opinion that counts."

Day 61

How We Got Milk and Eggs
and Knowing the Influence of Others

Relationships can make people far better than they ever would be.

They can make us far worse than ever too.

People influence us for good and for bad in our lives. Part of the reason may be just that we are relational beings and so our relationships always affect us so much.

The truth is we are not islands. If we think we're not affected by others, we are wrong. Thinking we are islands can lead us to let our guard down and not see how dangerous relationships could be. This thinking may be what keeps us from seeking out and finding solid fellowship and good influences.

For some, adding a good influence or removing a bad influence or two may be the one thing that makes all the difference in their life.

There really needs to be a lifelong pursuit of surrounding ourselves with all kinds of good relationships that lead us to where we need to be.

Rather than islands, we're more like plants and need the sunlight, soil, water… interconnected with all that is going on around us.

We are influenced by others!

Internalize this:

> **As iron sharpens iron, so one person
> sharpens another.**
>
> **Proverbs 27:17**

"Keep an eye on that guy!"

A bunch of guys will go to a stadium without shirts. Each with a different letter painted on their chest. It spells out P-A-N-T-H-E-R-S. They have a great time. Everyone loves it.

But no one just goes to the stadium with no shirt and the letter R on their chest. And, if so, would security even allow this? Well, if they do, security would keep an eye on shirtless R freak in row 27 seat F.

They would be radioing back and forth about R guy. "Where did he go? The bathroom? Okay. You wait outside the door until R guy is back in his seat." This same "freak" is celebrated so long as he's got those other letters somewhere near him.

Who is around us makes a big difference. I think this is how milk and eggs must have first been tried. Two guys standing around. One says, "Why don't you go over to that cow. Grab it by the teats. Whatever comes out, you drink."

The other guy is like, "What!!?" Then the first guy adds, "I dare you. I double dog dare you. Here's a pail." His friend responds, "Okay. I will do that if you will eat the next thing that comes out of that chicken's bottom!"

Now we have milk and eggs. We have cream and cheese and desserts and good breakfasts ever since! It's all about influence sometimes.

Know relationships are a way people become even better than they would ever be or worse than they could ever imagine. Know the influence of others and all relationships are so powerful.

Watch the influence of others and have some really close people to you who always lead you to what is good. Have relationships of all kinds that constantly make you better. You may need to limit some negative ones too.

Know iron sharpens iron. Know you are not an island!

Watch your "sunlight, soil, and water".

Reading: Titus 2:1-8

"Behind every great person are great relationships."

Day 62

Two Step-Brothers on Different paths and Charting a Good Financial path

No matter what anyone says or pretends to believe, money is important. It is important to me, to you, to everyone. Period!

It's important since it takes money to provide for our family, enjoy certain things in the world God made, and give to others. These things all matter a lot! So we need to live like money's important. Not in greed, envy or any of these things. These things come out of the love of money. That's not how you treat money as important.

Rather, the call is to work hard, plan ahead, spend wisely, stay out of unwise debt, get trained and educated, use our skills and innovation, and give generously! This is how we treat money as important! There are lots of people in life who are masters of money and their finances by doing these things. Others are financial disasters by ignoring these very same things. Being a master of money and of finances should be a very important priority of our life.

Managing our finances well may be a big part of accomplishing all God wants for us and others!

Internalize this:

> **Whoever has will be given more; whoever does not have, even what they have will be taken from them.**

> **Mark 4:25**

A letter to remember!

In 1850, Abraham Lincoln wrote a letter responding to John D. Johnston, his step-brother. Johnston was requesting money from Lincoln. Prior to this letter, Lincoln had just given Johnston money on a few occasions. Not this time. Here's how the letter reads in part:

Dear Johnston:

Your request for eighty dollars I do not think it best to comply with now. At the various times when I have helped you a little you have said to me, "We can get along very well now"; but in a very short time I find you in the same difficulty again.

Now, this can only happen by some defect in your conduct. What that defect is, I think I know… you are an idler. I doubt whether, since I saw you, you have done a good whole day's work in any one day… It is vastly important to you, and still more so to your children, that you should break the habit.

What I propose is, that you shall go to work, "tooth and nail"… and, to secure you a fair reward for your labor, I now promise you, that for every dollar you will, between this and the first of May, get for your own labor… I will then give you one other dollar.

Now, if you will do this, you will be soon out of debt, and, what is better, you will have a habit that will keep you from getting in debt again. But, if I should now clear you out of debt, next year you would be just as deep in as ever.

Affectionately your brother,
Lincoln

Notice we all know of Abraham Lincoln, but almost no one knows of John D. Johnston. It may be in part that one mastered money and one was enslaved by it. Our success or failure, our being known or unknown, our helping society or hurting it, may all come down to how we are with money.

Do not say as many do, "money doesn't matter". Know how important money really is in life. Work hard and plan ahead, be responsible, innovative, stay out of unwise debt, get trained and educated and everything else that goes into being a master of your finances!

Know counting money as important and handling money well will make a huge difference for you.

Master your finances!

Reading: Proverbs 6:1-15

"Money is important after all."

Day 63

April Fool's Day as a Favorite Holiday and the Importance of Rest

Rest is needful.

Too much work, too much routine and we will become dull, crabby, neglect our family, and just live apart from the joy of our heavenly Father. On the seventh day, God rested. But we often neglect to rest. If we do take time off, we sometimes don't really rest in our hearts and lives.

There are two kinds of stress, good and bad. Good stress is called "eustress". It keeps us alert, helps us get things done. We need it. It comes from normal living. Bad stress is called "distress". This is stress that works against us. It leads to breakdown and trouble. It also leads to doing lots of things that are not at all what God wants.

We are called by God to the good kind of stress, the eustress, but to avoid all distress. Much distress can come from a lack of rest in our lives.

It has even been observed that time off doesn't lower our productivity but increases it. When you take a break, you end up accomplishing more since you are refreshed and ready to do more. You just get more done in less time. So, all the while you will not take a break, you're not even getting more done.

God has designed all things to function best with occasional rest. Even the human heart that you would think is going all the time is actually taking a brief rest after every beat. We should never think that somehow we will overcome how everything has been designed and be able to skip rest.

We will not. We will just get filled with distress.

Internalize this:

> In my distress I called to the Lord; I called out to my God. From his temple he heard my voice; my cry came to his ears.

> 2 Samuel 22:7

I think you can tell a lot about a person by their favorite holiday. You know, usually someone will go with Christmas or Thanksgiving. But then there are all those other answers out there.

I once had a neighbor who went all out every year for Halloween. Now, I can see that for kids but not for him. He had a fog machine and sound effects and all. This was his holiday. I felt like asking him, "Are you alright? You know, things going well at work… at home?"

For some it seems their holiday is April Fool's Day. This isn't good. We must agree this is a strange holiday, a sad excuse for one. What kind of day is it when you can do just about anything and, when it's all over, get away with it saying "April Fools!" Your neighbor lets all the air out of your tires. After watching you freak out yells over, "April Fools" and you're supposed to be like, "Oh yeah… got me… ha, ha… happy holiday to you too." Now, if there is anyone at work for whom this is their favorite holiday, call in sick. Stay home.

Columbus Day is a bit thin as a holiday too. I mean, Columbus found this hemisphere by mistake. He didn't even know where he was going or where he was when he got here… and we take a day off for it.

I think this is a great interview question. You ask, "What's your favorite holiday?" If they say like Christmas, Thanksgiving, Easter, or Veteran's Day you should be fine. If they say Halloween, April Fools, or Columbus Day, they're out.

Well, whatever your favorite holiday, remember the importance of time off and rest. Are you overdoing it? Walking in distress? Is it leading you astray from the things God wants? Making you less productive and capable? Take the needed breaks.

Enjoy those holidays and every other break. Follow His example.

Know you're better rested up.

Like everything else God made.

Reading: Psalm 116:1-13

"Take a holiday from distress."

Day 64

Flunking Out of School
and Giving it Your All in Life

You are gifted!

The Bible tells us that all of us have talents and gifts.

The big difference is only in how much we use our talents. This one thing can affect the outcome of your life greatly. We see all this in the parable of the talents that Jesus tells in the gospels. In it, you will see that all people have talent. That's not the issue.

In the parable though, only two people use the talents in a profitable way. They both create a great return on investment when they do.

A third guy buries his talent and gets reamed by the giver of the talents. He too, the parable continues, could have created yield from his talent – but he chose not to.

This is not a 'haves' and 'have nots' world when it comes to talents. But, it is a bit like that when it comes to how much we use our talents. Some do, many don't.

Of the two who used the talents they had, God said…

… "Well done."

Internalize this:

> **Well done, good and faithful servant!**
> **You have been faithful with a few things;**
> **I will put you in charge of many things.**
>
> **Matthew 25:21**

A brilliant mind scorned.

I had a roommate in college who was brilliant. In fact, I think he scored a near perfect score on his SATs to get into college. It's not every day you ask a guy how he did on his SATs and he can say something like "missed one".

You play chess with someone like that and the match lasts a few minutes. Just great!

I really feel had Einstein been in college with us at the time, he would have been coming over for tutoring on Physics from my roommate. He would have been like, "Help me. I just can't figure this stuff out!" and leave satisfied. The Wright brothers could've come to him for advice on making planes. Would have saved them a lot of those trial and errors we always see on film.

This is the kind of guy that always ruined the curve for everyone else. You know. If the highest grade is an 80, everyone goes up 20. Not so helpful when the top score is his 108.

However, one thing he lacked was a desire to use his talents well. Eventually, it all caught up with him and he failed out of college. This was a particularly difficult thing since his mother was on the university's staff. That meant he only had to pay half the normal tuition. If he wanted to get back in, I believe he had to wait about a year… and the half-price tuition deal was history.

It's amazing but true that success will not necessarily always go to the most talented people. Some of these will do well. Some will not.

Know that success comes to the person who uses whatever skills they have to the utmost. These are the ones who produce and invent and inspire.

Know that in God's economy all of us have been given enough latent talent to greatly bless the world.

Apply your gifts! And know He will say…

… "Well done!"

Reading: Matthew 25:14-30

**"Success does not come to the talented,
but the ones who use the talent they have."**

Day 65

A Drill, an 18 Year-Old,
and Contending for the Faith

Ever climbed a "why" tree?

It usually happens in a conversation with a toddler or someone just a bit older.

> "Why are peas green?"
> "Why does Saturn have a ring?"
> "Why do cats purr?"

It's predictable, never-ending, and requires a lot of patience (a sense of humor helps, too). It's just how we're designed – we want to know who, what, where, when, how… and especially, why.

As a Christian, you're going to want to be able to answer people's questions about faith and eternal matters. It's your calling. God says in the book of Jude, "Contend for the faith that was once for all entrusted to the saints."

They've got questions, and they need answers. These questions are like distracting pebbles in a shoe or maybe like big road barriers standing between God and them. These pebbles and barriers need to be removed. It all may be the one thing standing in their way.

Learning more and more, preparing ourselves for these opportunities, is just what God is calling us to do. To answer questions well, it takes soundness in our own faith, holding to the Scriptures with all that you say.

And, love enough to do it.

Internalize this:

. **Always be prepared to give an answer to everyone who asks you to give the reason for the hope that you have. But do this with gentleness and respect.**

1 Peter 3:15

I was 19 years old, and I was going to get to the bottom of this – even if it took all night.

My cousin was visiting, and we were going to have a talk. Pat was 18, and I knew he'd recently "become a Christian". Since he had grown up going to church, he was a puzzle to me.

For the first 45 minutes, I just drilled this guy with the hardest questions I could think of about the Christian faith. He answered every one. Because he was able to answer all these questions, I then let him just talk after that. He told me everything else I needed to know over the next 45 minutes. It was the first time I ever really heard the gospel expressed in a way I understood it.

The next day, I accepted Christ into my life. My cousin's willingness and ability to answer my questions opened the door for him to share the whole gospel. It cleared away barriers I had from unanswered questions.

Sure you can't argue people into the kingdom. That's not the point. But, you can open the heart by speaking to the head, answering questions. That's the point. That's what he did. Many are ready for this. In fact, someone cannot embrace with their heart what their mind rejects. The mind must embrace it too. We can help with that.

If an 18 year old can do it, so can we. And, he had only been a Christian at that time for six months. Be ready yourself for the many opportunities that will come your way to guide people to God. Be in the Word and know it. Be prepared to lovingly give answers.

Know you may be removing the very obstacles that are keeping them from the faith. Know you may be leading them to a saving knowledge of Jesus Christ by your answers.

Get to their heart through their head.

Contend for the faith.

Reading: Philippians 1:3-11

> **"Sometimes you have to get to the heart
> by going through the head."**

Day 66

Zeke the Turtle Makes it Home
and How to Make it Home to Heaven

That's not how it works!

Often other religions don't talk about salvation or being saved from the penalty of sin at all. They deny sin, heaven, or a personal God altogether leaving there no need for salvation. When these religions do talk about salvation, they always talk about what works you need to do to be saved.

These works they say are necessary are always determined by them, what works they think must be done. These works may even change as time goes on. The amount of works is also determined by the religion and they often don't say what would be enough. This amount might also change each generation.

And what about people right on the border, if salvation were by works? Would they miss by one small work they didn't do or one little wrong thing they did? "Should not have cheated on that 5th grade math test!"

Christianity has a unique answer to all this. It says that the amount of works you need to do to be saved is zero. And this amount never changes. And, that's good because all we have really accomplished is zero anyway. The Bible says in Isaiah that all our righteous acts are as "filthy rags".

But, in Christ we are counted as if we have never sinned, a score of 100. By turning from our own self-effort and accepting Christ, we go from 0 to 100. His righteousness is given to us.

This is salvation by grace, the only way anyone is ever saved.

Internalize this:

> **Here I [Jesus] am! I stand at the door and knock. If anyone hears my voice and opens the door, I will come in and eat with him, and he with me.**

> **Revelation 3:20**

Zeke is a turtle that has had his 15 minutes of fame!

He was a beloved turtle by everyone in the family that had owned him for 31 years. But, one day, he got out of the house and was lost. The family panicked.

The search began in the neighborhood. They looked everywhere for Zeke. When they couldn't find him, the search widened. They put flyers up as far as two miles away. With everyone seeing the flyers, the search made it to the local news. Now everyone for several towns away knew to be looking out for the lost turtle.

There was even a reptile-sniffing dog on the hunt. Still Zeke never turned up. Then, after 30 days, when almost all hope had been lost, Zeke appeared. But he wasn't two miles away. He wasn't several towns over or anything at all like that. No. Zeke was just in the neighbor's backyard. Very close to the door he first walked out of.

Call the county-wide search off!

That's us! No we're not turtles, of course. But when we try to earn salvation by good works, we really get nowhere. Still in the back yard. Even less than that… zero steps when all is said and done.

Remember the two numbers: 0 and 100. Zero is our efforts. Filthy rags. One hundred is the perfect score we get if we are in Christ. The righteousness of Christ is indeed 100.

Don't try for salvation by good works and, in reality, leave God out. You get nowhere. Know salvation is by grace and live in the grace offered to you in Christ.

Decide on receiving Christ and what He's done for you.

Go from 0 to 100.

Reading: Romans 8:1-27

"Salvation is just a decision away."

Day 67

A Life-saving Night of Bowling and Accepting Only Christ's Perfection

Somebody once said, "Perfection is the enemy of greatness."

It's an interesting thought.

Perhaps, needing perfection can keep us from a lot of great things. Maybe we don't love our spouse or stay with them since they are not perfect. Maybe we don't accept ourselves since we're not perfect. Maybe we don't get more involved in church life since it's not perfect. Maybe we end up leaving our job since it's not perfect.

If any of these are the case, then perfection really is the enemy of greatness. Our relationship to our spouse, ourselves, our church, our job, can be great if we would not demand it to be perfect.

We cannot demand perfection of anyone, including ourselves. Perfection is not going to be in us or anything we do. It is in Christ. He alone is perfect. We have His righteousness, not our own.

The psalmist said, "To all perfection I see a limit, but your commands are boundless."

It's not that we accept sin as okay. Sin is anything but okay. Rather, we accept that we are fallen in a fallen world relying on grace. We extend grace and love to others, not this demand of perfection.

Then we can find greatness instead.

Internalize this:

> **God made him who had no sin to be sin for us, so that in him we might become the righteousness of God.**

> **2 Corinthians 5:21**

One lousy pin!!

Bill Fong of Texas once bowled an 899. That's right. Not just a 299 or near perfect game of 300. He bowled an 899. It was a near perfect series which would be three perfect games in a row, a 900. He bowled two perfect games then a 299.

There have been plenty of perfect games, but there have been only 21 known and official perfect series'… ever. Fong just missed doing that!

He had a crowd of well over 100 people watching after he bowled his first two perfect games. Everyone was breathless as each ball went down the lane in the third game. Some didn't want to make eye contact with Fong so they wouldn't mess him up.

In the third game, he bowled nine strikes in a row. When he got to that last frame he needed just one more strike. All fell except the 10 pin. It wobbled. It stayed up. 899. No perfect series. Much disappointment.

It was found out sometime afterward, that Fong actually had a stroke that night. It was coming on toward the end of the third game. He was dizzy later in the evening but no other symptoms that night. Tests revealed it later.

His doctor told Fong that if he had bowled that 900, he may well have had a much bigger stroke and died. Fong ultimately became grateful for missing perfection. It could have cost him his life.

Know the demand for perfection can take away an awful lot from all of us too if we let it. It may lead to a lot of bad marriages, low self-esteem, not being active at church, quitting a good job, and much more.

Let us realize the imperfect job, church, ministry, friends, and husband or wife is enough and walk in grace.

Do not let perfectionism keep you disappointed and destroy you.

Only Christ is perfect.

Reading: Psalm 119:89-96

"Perfection is the enemy of greatness."

Day 68

"Partially Obstructed View" and What Focus on God Will Do

The Bible talks a great deal about complete devotion to God, complete dedication. There are lots of reasons for this.

For one thing, He deserves that kind of attention, not some on-again off-again reaction. It also makes sense when you think of how much God loves us. If you loved someone so dearly, would you want a relationship that was on and off? Our call from God is simply the same.

What's more, it is this kind of devotion that really leads to deep growth. What power and change comes to our lives when we are completely dedicated to Him!

Isn't that what is meant by "Lord" anyway? That our devotion is on Him, allowing Him to guide us and be our God? You can't say someone is your Lord and then go and disobey some of the time.

So, by calling for complete devotion, God is calling for the only appropriate reaction we can give to a loving God. He is calling for what we really need for growth and our own spiritual well-being. And, He is calling that we make Him Lord of our life.

Behind it all, God is calling for complete devotion to Him because in His great love…

… He wants all of you.

Internalize this:

> **Let your eyes look straight ahead;**
> **fix your gaze directly before you.**
> **Give careful thought to the paths for your feet**
> **and be steadfast in all your ways.**
>
> **Proverbs 4:25-26**

"This pole!"

You know if you've ever gone to a game in a big stadium or arena that there are good seats and not so good seats. Then, even somewhere below 'not so good' there is the dreaded "Partially Obstructed View" seat.

This is the seat where you're behind a pole or something like that. When they built the place, they debated whether they should even put a seat there. They couldn't move the support beam so should they bother with the seat? They went with it.

When you're in that seat you're not exactly seeing what's going on. So, you're constantly asking the people you come with... "What just happened? I couldn't see. I'm sorry."

There's also a delay in your celebration because of this seat. Your team scores. Everyone in the arena is jumping up and cheering. Then about ten seconds later with everyone else quiet, they hear you say, "Yeah!" Everyone looks over at you now the only one standing. You look around and defend your delay, "I couldn't see! Obstructed view."

The seats you really want are the ones right by the bench of the entire basketball team. You want to be so close that when the coach points to a player towards the end of the bench to put him in the game, you think he might just kinda be pointing at you.

You say, "What, me coach? You want me to go in? Because I'm ready coach! Oh, what's that? You were actually pointing to the guy in the uniform next to me who is really on the team? Oh. Okay. Well, good call coach." You give him a big thumbs up. He never looks your way again.

So, what kind of seat are you in with God? End of the bench or behind the pole? Know focus on God means growth and success in Him. Know it means living where He is Lord. Realize it means treating this loving relationship the way it was meant to be.

Fix your gaze directly before you... directly on Him.

Reading: Hebrews 12:1-13

> ## "An unobstructed view is the only kind to have toward God."

Day 69

A Useless Tack Hammer
and Your Usefulness in Ministry

People need you. Lots of people do.

You are pivotal to the well-being of the body of believers. The church needs what you do. Without you, something is missing, something very important. That sure is what the Bible has to say about you and your calling. It likens all of us to a physical body. Each part is so important.

We cherish each part of our body and give every part the attention it must have to function well because it's so important.

Paul said, "There are many parts, but one body... The eye cannot say to the hand, 'I don't need you!'... If one part suffers, every part suffers with it; if one part is honored, every part rejoices with it."

You can see how important it really is then that you carry out your part. Your part is key. If you don't do it, it is lost. This must not happen. One part of a body is missing! We need all the parts.

We need you.

Internalize this:

> **Now you are the body of Christ, and each one of you is a part of it.**
>
> **1 Corinthians 12:27**

It was Father's Day, I believe, and we were going to do something very creative for my father.

The whole family was going to a hardware store and buying a tool box for my father. Then, we were all going to pick a tool and put that in the box.

When all is done, he would have a tool box filled with all the tools he really needed... well, so was the plan anyway.

There was one problem. As a six year old, or so, I had no idea what a good tool was to place in the box. How would I know? I never fixed anything... broke a lot of things.

Yes, I was a good breaker of things. If you needed something broken, I was your guy. But fixing things? Nah. So which tool? What do adults have in a tool box? Do they have hammers and pliers or forks and toothbrushes? I don't know. Now it was my turn to pick. In the end, my selection was not quite as bad as say a fork or a toothbrush, but it was close to that bad. I chose a tack hammer.

What? A tack hammer? Are you kidding me? Who needs a hammer for a tack? Why was that even in a hardware store? What was I thinking? Oh sure, the store had the great tools. It had the wrenches, the screwdrivers, and the levels. But I passed right over those. I went right to the tack hammer.

Now I'm sure it was a good tack hammer as tack hammers go. But it was a tack hammer. It had no actual use. It was not a pivotal part of a tool box. It hardly belonged in the store. No hardware store signs ever say, "We have new tack hammers!" No handy man has ever said, "Now where did I leave my tack hammer?"

Realize this though. When it comes to ministry, there are no "tack hammers" in the kingdom of God. In contrast, every "tool" is pivotal, every calling is essential.

Know your calling is essential to the well-being of the body of Christ. It is the pliers, the saw, the nails.

Live like it. Jump into ministry. Get your calling accomplished and all the body of Christ will be better for it.

Know that no one can replace you.

Reading: Ephesians 4:1-16

"Your ministry is unique. If you withhold it, something wonderful is lost.

Day 70

The Cure for Halitosis
and the Cure for Sin

Many things aren't what they seem.

This can certainly be the case with sin. There are a whole lot of misconceptions about it.

Some think sin is all the fun things in life you can't do. They think the people doing sinful things are often so happy and free. Others think sin is just an arbitrary rule or cultural norm. No big deal.

No. Sin is a violation of God's unalterable moral code. Not something less. It is very harmful. Not something better. Sin may have a passing pleasure but it's very momentary. In the end, it's destructive. Ultimately, it bites, it stings, it hurts, and it destroys.

So instead of embracing sin as if it's kind of okay or even good, the Bible urges us to stay far from it. "Pursue righteousness, faith, love and peace."

We bring great harm to our lives when we allow sin. The prophet Jeremiah once said, "Why bring such destruction on yourselves?"

Actually knowing this about sin and living like we know it makes us a wise person. It makes us wise, loving, holy… all the truly good things in life.

And in these things the psalmist said there is "fullness of joy".

Internalize this:

> **The thief comes only to steal and kill and destroy; I have come that they may have life, and have it to the full.**

> **John 10:10**

Sometimes, in the medical profession, things that sound like bad news are really good and things that sound like good news are really bad.

This happens with the diagnosis doctors give. It doesn't sound right. You get tested for a disease. The doctor comes back and tells you the test is positive. Not thinking, you rejoice. After all, that sounds good. It's positive. I like positive. No one wants negative right? In this case, actually, yes, you want negative... very much so. Negative is... well, positive.

Here's another example. I think if you tell people who don't know what the word means that you have a physical condition known as halitosis, they would assume it was a really bad thing.

Your friends would be like "Oh my goodness, that's awful. What can we do for you? Do you want us to send over some meals? We know a really good doctor. Maybe you should get a second opinion."

Your close relatives just break out in tears except your angry uncle who stands up and says, "Those doctors know nothing. I'm sure you're fine!" Your critical cousin just says, "Should've taken better care of yourself." Your church even holds a special prayer vigil for your recovery. The whole church comes out. Some begin fasting for you.

Of course, all you actually needed was... a mint. There's even a phobia about bad breath. Even this word sounds bad, halitophobia. You would think it's a fear of really scary things like tornadoes or getting shipwrecked or something like that. Nope, you are just afraid of a guy who had onions for lunch.

In the same way, it's important to know what sin really is and how harmful it will always be. Never mistake it for the carefree, fun lifestyle it's often portrayed to be. Never mistake it as an arbitrary, culturally based rule you can ignore.

Reject the "passing pleasure" of sin. Embrace purity, holiness, goodness! Pursue righteousness, faith, love, and peace.

Walk in "fullness of joy".

Reading: Romans 3:9-26

"Sin is ugly. Holiness is beautiful."

Day 71

"Run Out that Fly!"
and the Importance of Being Ready

Hope!

The believer should be abiding in great hope in their life at any given time. There should be a sense of great hope for the future since God is so great.

What a shame to miss out on something wonderful because we already gave in to what we thought would be next, something not so wonderful. We didn't appreciate all God was going to do. We lacked hope.

Sometimes we fail to prepare for the future because we just don't expect enough. We can become so complacent from no hope, so unprepared.

Having a sense of hope and readiness for great things is a part of planning and preparing. Like a farmer who sows their seed at the right time because they have hope in the harvest to come.

For the believer, tomorrow may be far different and far better than you ever thought. Knowing this will change how we live in the present. It will make us much more diligent, confident, joyful, expecting, and ready. All from hope in God.

No wonder we are called to abide these three, "faith, hope and love".

Internalize this:

> **Now to him who is able to do immeasurably more than all we ask or imagine, according to his power that is at work within us, to him be glory in the church and in Christ Jesus throughout all generations, for ever and ever! Amen.**

Ephesians 3:20

What's the deal with some of these baseball players not running out fly balls when they hit them?

Look, I know that outfielders in the Majors rarely miss the ones hit right to them, but for the batter to run out a fly in case the fielder misses seems like a pretty good thing to do.

Maybe it adds a little pressure to the fielder to catch the ball. Maybe it just gets the batter's blood pumping out there and they are better off either way. Hey, just for my sake, as I watch the play unfold and don't know the outcome… run the ball out. Run to first base. Run! You never know.

In fact, I once saw an outfielder miss the ball. It hit him in the head and bounced over the wall for a home run. Would the batter run it out then?!

It's the same thing with using two hands for the outfielders. The ball does pop out from time to time, I know that. Their other hand isn't doing anything anyway. Get it up by your glove and squeeze the glove after that ball goes in it. It's not complicated.

I once saw a ball bounce out of an outfielder's glove and the other fielder caught it. Now it shouldn't take two people. Use the second hand.

I wonder if there are some things that we've become lackadaisical over because we figure we already know the outcome too. We in essence are not running out those flies or using two hands since we figure these things won't matter. We're not hoping in God as we should. We expect too little from an almighty God.

Know the future God has is always better than you think. He does immeasurably more than all we ask or imagine. Be ready for this kind of future.

Let it show in your readiness, your planning, your joy, the way you plant seeds and wait for the harvest.

Expect great things to unfold as you are faithful to God since He is so great.

Abide faith, hope, and love.

Reading: 1 Thessalonians 5:1-23

"Never expect too little from an almighty God."

Day 72

A Boy Named Hamburger
and Having a Great Influence on Your Kids

Clearly the home you create for your kids is very important. There are so many negative influences out there for kids that having a great home life is critical.

It's not always easy. But when we as parents choose to fill our homes with love, joy, support, good relationships, and godliness, it's the best gift we can give our children.

These things stay with kids long into adulthood. They remember these things deep in their being. They become who they are largely as a result. Someone once thankfully said, "I remember my mother's prayers and they have followed me. They have clung to me all my life." How true!

Never is a person more impacted by what goes on around them, than when they are a child. What a great opportunity we have as parents to provide our kids with the exact environment they really need. This takes desire and leadership. Leadership because your children are not going to be telling you they want or need your influence. In fact, when they are teens, they are likely to tell you they don't want it.

They may say they only want their friends or the influence of many other things. We cannot follow their lead, but provide them with the influence they really need, the influence of a good home life and good relationship with their parents. In contrast to what so many may think, the greatest influence in the life of children is not their friends. No, far from it.

It is their parents.

Internalize this:

> **Train a child in the way he should go, and when he is old he will not turn from it.**

> **Proverbs 22:6**

Quick: What's your earliest memory?

Can you remember? Try. It was probably when you were around three or four. I can pinpoint mine, at least, I think, you know, as far as I can remember. It was just a very small thing. My family was sitting around a table trying to decide the name for my younger brother. I was just three years and four months old.

We went around the table each giving a name. As we went along, it got sillier and sillier. We began to really laugh together at that table. "How about... Hamburger?!" someone said.

Poor kid. Can't you just hear the name calling on that one? "Hey Hamburger, where's your ketchup and pickles?" They say that the name you give your child is your first gift to them. This would've been a lump of coal.

Why did this stick with me as my first memory? I've come up with a few reasons. I think just because it was a joyful experience with family togetherness. It was, in the end, so powerful that I remember it, even though I've forgotten millions of other moments.

Are you aware of the influence you truly do have? Do you seek to give your kids the godly influence they need in you as a parent? If you are not a parent yet, are you growing in faithfulness now so that when the time comes, you will already be a mature believer for your children?

Commit to being and bringing the best to your home. Know you'll create for your kids a vault of powerful, positive memories to draw from and help them become all they're meant to be.

Let your home be filled with all the things that a child really needs, that joy, that togetherness they will never forget.

Know this influence far exceeds any of their others.

Train up your child in the way they should go.

Reading: Ephesians 4:17-5:2

**"We can be making a lot of positive deposits
in our kid's memory banks."**

Day 73

A Genius with Generators and a Genius with Your Heart

If you get wheeled off to surgery, you sure hope the doctor knows exactly what they are doing.

It's a lot similar when we rest in the Lord and let him do "surgery" on our hearts, our minds, our very being.

We know we need healing and growth. We want to be certain we are in the hands of One who knows just what to do to bring about that change. That's what is so great about this kind of "surgery". We always know God will do just the right things, leading us exactly to the right path for healing.

What great assurance we can have. So much so, we can truly rest in the Lord and allow the surgery to take place. The more we can settle it in our minds that God really does know what to do with our broken hearts and hurting souls, the better off we will be, the more thorough the healing.

So we see that the saints in the Bible had full assurance that God would bring about the change we need. The psalmist said, "Lord my God, I called to you for help, and you healed me."

So we see that God calls us to complete assurance in His results throughout this whole process too.

We can always say that I called upon the Lord, and He heard.

Great physicians get results.

Internalize this:

> **To the only wise God be glory forever through Jesus Christ! Amen.**
>
> **Romans 16:27**

A genius at work!

There's a story told about an event in the life of Henry Ford, the founder of the Ford Motor Company.

One of the things that was so significant about Henry Ford was that, through assembly line mass production, he made the automobile affordable to many people. As the story goes, one day, that assembly line production came to a halt. Ford was losing thousands of dollars as time went on.

None of Ford's mechanics could seem to solve the problem. So, Ford turned to the inventor of the generators that were used in the plant, one of the greatest minds in the field of electricity, a man named Charlie Steinmetz.

Steinmetz had about ten patents in the field. He came and tinkered with the engines a bit, adjusting some wires here and some gauges there. Within a couple hours, the plant was up and running again. The assembly line production was back in process. Ford's profits again secured.

Then Ford received the bill from Steinmetz: $10,000. Ford thought that was crazy and wrote back, "Charlie, isn't this bill just a little high for a few hours of tinkering around with a few wires and switches?"

Steinmetz replied: "For tinkering around on the motors: $10. For knowing where to tinker: $9,990. Total $10,000." Ford promptly paid the bill.

Know this in the process of your spiritual growth: God has the remedy for your broken heart and unrenewed mind. He knows all you need at every given moment!

Know He is the only wise God. And what He does with you will be just right too. Rest in Him for growth.

Trust Him to heal you.

The genius Creator knows just where to "tinker" too.

Reading: Matthew 9:1-26

"The Great Physician always has the right cure."

Day 74

Being a Good 'Flipper'
and Knowing the Bible Well

Studying is not just for children.

Few people realize just how significantly we are called to know the content of the Bible. We are called to be great students of the Bible.

Just read what some of the greats said like Paul, "Study to show yourself approved unto God, a workman that needs not to be ashamed, rightly dividing the word of truth."

David: "I have hidden your word in my heart that I might not sin against you."

Peter: "Always be prepared to give an answer to everyone who asks you to give the reason for the hope that you have."

The Bible says that when we live our life by the Word, it is like building our house on the rock. But we must study the Word to do that. We are called to have the Bible as our authority. However, the Bible cannot really be our authority if we don't know what it says.

Study is a must for us to learn God's Word.

And, study leads to great ways of helping others know His Word too.

Internalize this:

> **Study to show yourself approved unto God, a workman that needs not to be ashamed, rightly dividing the word of truth.**

> **2 Timothy 2:15 (KJV)**

I'll never forget the first Bible study I ever attended as an adult. It was on my college campus in a musty, poorly lit room of a very old building.

To be honest, I wasn't sure I should enter at all.

I went with a friend of mine (safety in numbers) and we entered the room with fear and trepidation. When we got in, we realized we were going to be the only ones at this study, just us and the teacher. (Now I really wasn't sure I should've gone in!)

But, as a new believer, I had about a thousand questions to ask the Bible study leader. So, being the only ones there, this was my chance. I began asking all my questions. I was pleasantly surprised with what happened next. This guy didn't just answer the questions. He would flip right to the spot in the Bible where the question was answered.

He wouldn't even read the verses. I would ask. He would flip. Then he would point to the verse and have me read it. It was the exact answer to my question every time. This went on for a while. He was never at a loss. He just kept flipping and I kept reading.

As a new believer, I figured every believer who has been one for a time must be able to do that with the Bible. You know, just flip to the exact spot every time because they know the Bible so well. Sadly, I have found that this is not the case and that this guy was actually rare. It's rare but it shouldn't be.

Let us "study to show ourselves approved". Let us come to know the Bible well so that it is really our authority, so that we are really building our house on the rock with His Word hidden in our hearts. Let us be like the greats who knew the Bible well – Paul, David, and Peter, and make knowing His Word not so uncommon.

That guy eventually went on from that musty old building to become the team chaplain for the New York Giants of the NFL and the New York Yankees of Major League Baseball to this day.

I wonder what it's like to read the sports page with this guy. I ask him who won last night's game. He flips, I read. Right answer every time.

May we be able to flip and find and see all the life changes and opportunities this will bring us as well.

Reading: Ephesians 1:1-23

"The Bible can't be our authority unless we know what it says."

Day 75

Two People Dead at church
and Being Alive in Worship

Empty.

That's how many experience church. Stained glass. Choir robes. Three points and a poem from the pastor. Then a friendly handshake on your way out the door. That's it, the fulfillment of an obligation for some. Just leave your coat on and hope to get out early. What a miss!

Instead, we are to meet with God Himself, being moved by Him. Having Him do open-heart surgery on us right then and there, leaving us transformed – leading us to change the world around us.

But some settle for a cheap imitation, the appearance of "doing" church. They exchanged the experience of God with the experience of going to church. One is fulfilling, the other is empty. One pleases God, the other displeases Him.

Jesus warned about just going through the motions or just having a religion instead of knowing Him. He said, "These people honor me with their lips, but their hearts are far from me."

There are nominal Christians and church goers. Then there are those on-fire Christians who meet with God.

What a difference!

Internalize this:

> **Therefore, I urge you, brothers and sisters, in view of God's mercy, to offer your bodies as a living sacrifice, holy and pleasing to God – this is your true and proper worship.**

> **Romans 12:1**

Now that's a church service! One day, two people, Ananias and Sapphira, fell dead in the middle of a church service. They lied to God and were struck dead by Him. It's recorded in Acts 5.

What if that happened at your church? Think you'd have anyone willing to come as your guest next week? You drive home from church, pull into your driveway. There's your neighbor, trimming his hedges. He looks up and asks how your service went. You dread the question thinking about those dead bodies.

Maybe you've been trying to get him to come to church. Now you're sure he won't come. You'd probably want to cushion what you had to say by talking about everything else that happened. "The hand bell choir was spot on! Nice white gloves too. And, they had this delicious lemon layer cake after service that was to die for... oh, and speaking of death..."

Reluctantly you tell him what happened. I think you might be surprised at how your neighbor would actually respond. He might say, "WOW. Now I've never heard of anything like that. Your God is really real. You guys aren't messing around over there. I want to be a part of THAT. What time's the service?"

You're like, "What?!" Why? It's not the death part they want, of course. What people need is to see God is alive and active. That's what they do not see at many churches and at many services. That's what they'll seek out. The early church really did grow right?

Now your church would catch on and put something on its sign like, "Two people were struck dead by God last week. Come in and see what happens next." Now there's a sign that will draw.

Know there's no point in settling for "playing church" and trying to get others to come out for that either. Instead, we can have an on-fire, all-out, dynamic, and powerful experience with God at church. Come to church to really encounter God. Commit to not playing church.

Know we need Him not an empty church life. Know it's what others need too.

And invite them to this!

Reading: 1 Kings 18:22-39

"There is a great gulf between empty religion and an encounter with God."

Day 76

Paying a $1 Debt
and Having our Eternal Debt Paid

When we sin, we incur a debt to God. Now with many debts we incur, we can pay it ourselves. So, for a financial debt, we can eventually catch up and pay what we owe. The debt we owe to God through our sin is not like that. It's a debt we cannot pay ourselves. It's too great.

Some try to pay the debt by doing a lot of good works… not gonna happen. Someone has said that doing good works is a lot like rearranging the furniture on the Titanic. The problem is much bigger than that.

You still owe.

Some get more religious to pay the debt, following empty, made up rules apart from God. More of what does not work won't work either.

You still owe.

Some try to deny sin altogether. "That's just being negative", they may say. Denying you have a debt will never wipe it away.

You still owe.

But Christ paid the debt we cannot pay and He paid it in full. What an amazing work by God who saw our desperate need and met it by His own blood on the cross. By His death, we can be debt-free.

And no longer owe.

Internalize this:

> **He forgave us all our sins, having canceled the charge of our legal indebtedness, which stood against us and condemned us; he has taken it away, nailing it to the cross.**
>
> **Colossians 2:13-14**

What's the interest on that?!

There was a touching news story of an older gentleman who got a parking ticket in 1946 for $1. Soon after, he got a money order for $1 to pay the ticket. But, he forgot to send it in.

About 60 years later, the man now 86 years old, found the $1 money order in his house. He realized only then that he had never paid the ticket. So as to add no further delay, hey, 60 years was enough, the man sent in the $1 money order after all that time.

With it, he wrote a letter to the police department of the town where he got the ticket explaining the delay in paying. After the police department received the letter and $1, they framed the money order and put it on display, touched by the sentiment.

When asked about it, the man said, "At my age, when I go out of here, I don't want to owe anyone a dime." We all want to owe God nothing too. But, only Jesus enables us to leave here not owing God a dime. Otherwise we owe big time.

Know that we really do have a debt owed to God. We are all sinful.

Accept Christ into your life if you haven't. Know that in Christ, the "charge of legal indebtedness" is removed. Know it has been nailed to the cross.

Know it's not about good works or empty religion or anything else. Do not deny the debt either. If so, you will still owe.

Leave here the only way you can be debt free…

… in Christ.

Reading: Matthew 27:27-54

"Leave this earth debt free –
leave with Christ."

Day 77

Last at the Church Buffet and Being First with Others

They say that the business world often runs like this: Do unto others before they do it unto you.

Hmmm. No wonder 5:00 pm seems like forever to get to and everyone is seeking to retire early.

Now kids often act this way. The rule in the playpen and playground seems to be "What's mine is mine and what's yours is mine."

Ultimately life really doesn't work that way. In fact, I think it's designed to hurt you if you try to live me-first! We are called to put away childish things. We are to be the servant and the servant is to be last in the sense that they really care about others. What a concept!

We are called in Scripture to consider other's needs "more important than our own." We're to look out for others and love them. This is the way the world is designed to run best. I bet any business would do better, with a deeper profit margin, if they looked out for others first instead of following the me-first principle. I think they would end up ahead of the competition.

I think kids in a playground would get a whole lot more fun out of it all if sharing were the rule of the day!

And, in applying this principle to our life, we and everyone around us, would end up much better off too.

Internalize this:

> **Carry each other's burdens, and in this way you will fulfill the law of Christ.**

> **Galatians 6:2**

It's interesting going last at the church buffet.

Others have already gone through the line. They come up to you and say, "Oh, you have got to try Frannie's three meat lasagna. Yum!" You go down the line and you see a big empty tray that says "Frannie" on the bottom but no lasagna. Sadly, you end up with the broccoli dish.

Then someone else comes up to you. "When you come to the desserts, make sure you get some of Marie's chocolate cake. Gotta have it." You get to the dessert section. Again, you see an empty plate with Marie's name on it. One of the plates has a little chocolate frosting on it though. You pick up the plate. You lick it. Someone says, "What are you doing?" You say, "I missed Frannie's lasagna and Marie's chocolate cake so BACK OFF." You end up with fruit for dessert.

So, now you sit down with your broccoli dish and fruit. You're next to the guy who went through the line first. He says, "Oh, you're dieting. Great. I'm all for you. Keep it up. All things are possible with God!" You see two helpings of lasagna on his plate. You take half when he is not looking.

At the end of the day, Marie's thankful that not only did everyone eat her cake but that she even got her plate back washed (so she thinks)! And, Frannie was glad to see two guys fighting over her… well, over her lasagna, anyway.

It may feel this way, last is last, that you'll be the one with the broccoli and fruit if you don't shove your way around. It may feel that way at work, at home, or even in the playground. But, know me-first is not the way to get ahead!

Know those who care for others and love are really going to be first. It is God's design, how it will work best for everyone.

Watch out for others. Seek to serve. Really care. Really love.

The last are first.

Reading: 1 Corinthians 13:1-13

"Love and care first puts you first with others."

Day 78

"A Plane Hit My House"
and Trusting God's Protective Hand

Some are good at survival in the rugged outdoors. Some shouldn't even be camping!

But a trusting believer is going to be good at survival in life. This is so since the believer is being watched over by a heavenly Father who has their very life and well-being in His hands. What can happen to us apart from what God allows?

Nothing.

So come flood, fire, persecution, or loss, the believer survives since God enables them through and over anything that comes their way.

The psalmist once put it this way, "With your help I can advance against a troop; with my God I can scale a wall."

Then, not only that, but having survived the difficult thing, we can say we are even stronger still. If God can make a cat to always land on its feet, I can only imagine what He can do with us!

In the end, the believer is strong in the strength of God's might doing what He calls us to do, having survived it all.

God says of us, "Stand he will, for the Lord is able to make him stand."

Praise be to God who is able to keep us from stumbling.

Internalize this:

> **To him who is able to keep you from stumbling and to present you before his glorious presence without fault and with great joy – to the only God our Savior be glory, majesty, power and authority, through Jesus Christ our Lord, before all ages, now and forevermore! Amen.**
>
> **Jude 1:24-25**

"My dog ate my homework."

It's funny to think that at some point, somebody probably actually tried that excuse for missing their homework. And, since it was the first time, they probably got away with it. Teacher is like, "Oh my! That's awful. Is the dog okay? Take a few days to redo that assignment and go make sure your dog is better."

Now say the same exact thing and you are thrown out of class. The excuse is old. I know of a guy, though, who had a great new excuse for missing his homework. A small plane actually crashed into his house while he was doing his homework.

The house was almost completely destroyed. In fact, 95% of the house was nothing but black char. The guy doing his homework was in that little 5%, that half a room, and he escaped injury entirely.

His great excuse would go like this: "Yeah, that's right, I didn't finish my homework... because A PLANE HIT MY HOUSE!" There is no comeback by the teacher for that! Teacher just says, "You have as long as you want to make it up. Get out of here."

Maybe someday this excuse will become what is old hat just not now. But, could you imagine how the guy felt coming out of his house, turning around to look at it and seeing what he just survived?

This is a picture, of sorts, I would say, of the faithful Christian. There may be giant catastrophes that will go on in their life perhaps, but God said He will cause us to survive, that nothing will take us down that God does not allow.

Be at peace, trust God in the storms. Know we are even better for it every time. Stay faithful to Him knowing that no matter what comes your way, you will stand...

... for the Lord is able to make you stand.

Reading: Psalm 69:1-18

"A believer is always a survivor in the Lord."

Day 79

Avoiding Raw Egg and Finding Joy in Fellowship

"Why go to church if I can just worship at home!?"

Many say things like that, but the reason that Christian fellowship is important should be clear. We simply need to look around at how God has designed the whole world. We can know that we are better together than we would ever be apart.

Take an orchestra for example. One part here and one part there does not a symphony make!

Some have said it's like logs on a fire. One log alone and the fire may die out. Many logs together and the flame burns for hours. What a difference!

Food is similar. Eat the same thing over and over and over and well, you don't want it anymore. Your body craves variety in food since our palate was designed that way. We also only get the right nutrients in variety.

Believers are the same way. We are not all that good separate, but we are mighty and powerful in Christ when together.

We gain perspective, wisdom, peace, joy, and everything else good when together. We lack all those things when separate.

Just like orchestras, fires, and food.

Internalize this:

> **How good and how pleasant it is when brothers live together in unity!**
>
> **Psalm 133:1**

"Yum!"

I used to love when my mom was baking something and she let me lick the bowl. This is probably true of every kid. One reason is that I don't think moms really know how much can be in the bowl. Another reason is that they definitely do not know how much can be on those electric mixer beaters. And, because of that mixer it was so creamy and good!

Then even if you got all that, you still get to have whatever she bakes. By the time everything's baked, she seemingly has forgotten you already licked your way to a couple portions.

But you know, it was a little different years ago when there were no mixers. Moms used to take the bowl of batter and grab it like you would when you put someone in a headlock. Then with only a spoon, she would mix the living daylights out of those ingredients.

From all that stirring, she had a right arm that could take you out! Occasionally, because it was not mixed as well without the mixer, you would get a taste of raw egg or something. But, you didn't say a thing.

Yea, she might have looked all sweet with her apron with flour on it, but don't cross her. With that right arm, she could mess you up! She already knew how to get someone in a headlock.

It is at these times we are reminded that some things just function much better together. Know that believers are like these ingredients, better together.

Be like a really creamy mix from the mixer. Know that fellowship is just like orchestras, logs on fires, food, and so much more.

Avoid being separate with sayings like, "I can just worship at home." "The church is just full of hypocrites."

Be in fellowship with other believers.

Know how good and pleasant it is!

Reading: 3 John 1:1-11

**"Many things are just better together –
like believers."**

- 158 -

Day 80

A New Heart through Surgery and a New Heart through Christ

Alive again!

The Lord Jesus Christ said he would transform our hearts from hearts of stone to hearts of flesh.

He would repair our hearts. They would be made completely new by Him.

But so often, we don't live like our hearts are repaired. We aren't really letting them beat again.

We can live as if they are still broken by all the wounds over our life, all the disappointments, all the hurts, all the worry, all the feelings of guilt.

We can be living as if our hearts are still like stone. We are cold to others, to God, and the whole world around us. We live as dead when really, we're alive.

We could be loving God and others deeply, tender to needs, free of guilt, full of joy, and hope.

You know, with hearts of flesh.

We need to step into the healing our hearts have in Christ.

He repaired our hearts so they'll beat again.

Internalize this:

I will give you a new heart and put a new spirit in you; I will remove from you your heart of stone and give you a heart of flesh.

Ezekiel 36:26

There is a story told, reportedly true, of a minister who had a friend. This friend was a heart surgeon.

The minister asked his surgeon friend if he could watch him do surgery in person. The surgeon agreed but said you have to stay in the corner and you can't say anything. Agreed (but that second part being a little difficult for some ministers)!

As the surgery went on, it appeared toward the end to not be going well. The surgeon repaired the heart but it didn't begin to beat again. The minister began to be concerned that maybe he was witnessing his friend perform an unsuccessful surgery and the patient wouldn't make it.

Then the surgeon went over to the head of the patient and said to her, "Your heart has been repaired. Tell it to beat again." Apparently she could still subconsciously hear and could tell her heart to beat again. Immediately after, her heart began beating.

The surgery was a success!

So often, we are just like this patient. We have had our heart fully repaired by Christ but it is not beating. We have not told it to beat again.

We treat our hearts as if they are hearts of stone. We are not loving again. We are not laughing again. We are dead.

Let yourself love again. Let yourself laugh again. Cast aside a heart of stone. Be alive again with your new heart of flesh.

Be filled with hope and joy… all the things that come from a heart that is repaired.

Overcome all the disappointments, the regrets, the feelings of guilt and remorse, the hurts…

…and tell your new, repaired heart to beat again.

Reading: Ezekiel 36:26-37:14

**"Tell your heart
to beat again."**

Day 81

Guided Through Hot Lava
and Having God's Guidance to Heaven

Imagine you're lost in the woods.

You have no way out. Then you run across two people. One looks like he has been lost in the woods longer than you. He smells, he's dirty, he has a giant beard. He hasn't eaten in a while.

He looks at you with some of the last strength he has left and says, "The way out is that way" pointing to his right.

But standing next to him is the Park Ranger. He has a perfectly pressed Park Ranger uniform on, his name on the left chest. He has a truck that looks like it can go anywhere, complete with zebra stripes.

He looks at you and says, "No, the way out of these woods is to the left. Hop in. I'll take you out."

Many in the world are listening to the man who has been in the woods longer than they are on how to get to heaven. They are trying good works, empty religion, human-made philosophy to get out. And, there are plenty of lost people offering up this cheap advice… like blind guides.

But, when you are lost, you don't ask the lost how to get out. Instead you ask the one who has never been lost, the Lord Jesus Christ. Christ has told us that the way to heaven is only by His death.

The Savior knows the way out of the woods.

The rest are blind guides.

Internalize this:

> **Lord, to whom shall we go? You have the words of eternal life.**

> **John 6:68**

"They allow that?"

Ever notice the laws in other countries can be a lot more lax than around here? I mean you can do things that we would outlaw as very unsafe. Here we have laws and fines for jay-walking.

My son and I were once in Guatemala. Guatemala has beautiful volcanoes. You know, active, live volcanoes spewing out molten lava that drips down the sides. Last I checked, lava is HOT.

So, I was a bit surprised to find out you are actually allowed to climb the volcanoes and check them out, lava and all. Here, we would have giant fences up saying "Danger. Keep Out."

There? They will give a guided tour up the volcano complete with bagged lunch. Well… with the right guide that is. And people are going up there all the time. Okay, so my son and I went on the tour. Sure enough we were right there with the lava. You could reach out and touch it, that close. Again, the difference was… the right guide.

In the end, we had the time of our lives going up, and, thankfully, back down the volcano. How much more significant is following the right guide when it comes to life and heaven. How seriously wrong it would be to follow a foolish, blind guide.

Let the Lord be your guide showing you the way to get to heaven – that you get there by His death, if we believe on Him.

Reject the blind guides as what they really are. Reject empty philosophy, false religion, or good works.

Go with the "Park Ranger". Go with the one who really has the "words of eternal life".

Go with Jesus.

Reading: Matthew 15:1-20

"When you are lost, you don't ask the lost the way out."

Day 82

Running into an Immovable Tree and Running into God's Will

"How can I know God's will for my life?"

This is one of the most asked questions by believers.

The reality is, there is one surefire way to make certain you find and fulfill God's will for your life. It's not mysterious or complicated. It's simply wanting His will above all else.

If you really want God's will above all else, you'll find it. God's will is not some slippery, hard-to-get kind of thing. The reason is that if you truly seek Him, He will guide you. He will be with you to lead you exactly where you need to go if you're open to it.

Sure, a lightning bolt would be nice. Or a deep, thunderous voice coming from the sky:

"Get married to David."
"Do the sound ministry at your church."
"Buy the Honda."

But we know God's will isn't usually revealed that way. But that doesn't mean it won't come through loud and clear in the end to the open heart. It comes to us a lot of the time, seemingly by chance – and even in the midst of indecision and frustration. But, if Christ is Lord, His will comes.

After all, He is our Good Shepherd and Heavenly Father.

Internalize this:

> Do not conform to the pattern of this world, but be transformed by the renewing of your mind. Then you will be able to test and approve what God's will is – his good, pleasing and perfect will.
>
> Romans 12:2

That's gotta hurt!

One day we were out playing football in the street, shirts versus skins (you know, one team takes off their shirts to differentiate from the other team and plays shirtless – these are the 'skins').

The street had trees on either side so there were many immovable objects around that you really didn't want to run into. Well, sure enough a pass was thrown way to the side. My friend ran out to catch it, eyes up at the ball.

SMACK! Right into one of those trees. It was definitely immovable. Just ask my friend. Even worse, my friend was "skins" that day. He said, "I'm fine. I'm fine." The entire front of his body said otherwise.

Ever worry that life might happen that way to you? You're going through life, striving to do God's will, keeping your eyes on Him… when suddenly, SMACK! You hit an immovable object you didn't expect, and miss His will.

Won't happen the same way a small child holding hands with his mom or dad won't suddenly smack into a tree. Won't happen the same way a sheep won't just fall into a pit with the shepherd right by its side.

If you're truly focused on Christ and His Word, know you can trust your Good Shepherd, your Heavenly Father. Know your Lord knows how to guide you and He will.

Let this kind of certainty fill your life. Fully trust in the ability of God to provide and lead you in His will. Want His will above all else. Make it your highest priority and deepest focus. Then know you have His will.

Know chance is not really chance, but the hand of God. Know it will not be bolts of lightning to reveal it. It will just be.

No trees for you.

Reading: Psalm 127

"If the Lord is your God, it will be harder to miss His will than to find it."

Day 83

A Disarming Bike Basket
and a Disarming Adversary

Not everything that glitters is gold.

It's very true that not everything that looks good and helpful actually is. In fact, the Bible even says many false teachers will look genuine. Even the devil will show himself as an angel of light.

Paul said, "For such men are false apostles, deceitful workmen, masquerading as apostles of Christ. And no wonder, for Satan himself masquerades as an angel of light."

It's one thing to be taken by something clearly evil. We see it coming a mile away. It is quite another when that something is coming at you disguised as something good. This adds a new element of danger. And the devil always seeks to use deception as part of his warfare.

Many people are carried away by such teachers and disguises as these. False teachers may have degrees or be high up in religion. They may be intelligent, fervent, charming and all that. They may have a big following too. This is disarming of the true danger that may lie beneath what appears to be there.

We are called to a higher and better level of discernment. We can test what is said and done and see if it really matches the Word of God. It must really lift up Jesus Christ.

We are called not to get taken by glitter as if it is gold.

Internalize this:

> **Dear friends, do not believe every spirit, but test the spirits to see whether they are from God.**

> **1 John 4:1**

I was riding around with my parent's bike one day. It really was my parent's bike. I mean it's made for safety not speed. One of its distinguishing features is a basket on the front. Now do you realize how disarming having a big basket on the front of your safety bike is?

People start saying "Hi" to you and all. They figure a guy with a basket will definitely say "Hi" back. After all, this guy has a basket on the front of his bike. He's got to be friendly. He's got to want a "Hello". He probably needs a "Hello" really.

Maybe all these people saying "Hi" try to figure what I put in the basket too. Stuff like a little rain jacket in case it starts to drizzle. Maybe veggies I just bought at a market.

I started to think that with a big basket on my bike, I could get away with just about anything. I could ride my bike right up to a bank, ask them for all the money they have and they would just give it. After all, they would say, "He's got a basket on the front of his bike. This guy has to be alright."

The basket would even come in handy to hold all that cash as I leave. Then as I'm riding away, some of the money flying out of my basket, they say… "What a nice man. He has a basket."

Well, my bike and basket aren't quite that powerful to disarm. But we can be very disarmed by many things that lead us off the path of what it true and right. Those things are that powerful.

Instead of being duped by false teachers, be discerning and alert and sober. Do not be caught off-guard and deceived. Be on the alert for the angel of light and the false teachers who follow him.

Test the spirits. See what really matches with God's Word. See if they really exalt Christ by all they do and say.

Know all that glitters is not gold.

Reading: The book of Jude

**"The most dangerous influences
are the ones disguised."**

Day 84

King Kong on Your First Day and Finding Deep, Inner Growth

Sponges.

That's pretty much the best way to describe how we grow up. When we're little, we soak up everything going on around us. We believe so much of what we see, what we hear or think we see and hear – especially about ourselves. Not much discriminating between what's true and what's false, mostly because at that point we can't discern well what's accurate and what's not.

The thing is, since you took all of this in as a little kid, much of it is now buried deep in your being. Now, as you seek to stretch and grow, you face a process of digging deep down.

It's a big task. It involves uncovering some "facts" buried in your heart and mind, taking a look, and deciding whether they're even true. If they're not, you can replace them with what is true.

This takes time, commitment, and not a little courage. The moment you choose to go deep, you're likely to see some stuff that's… just ugly. You may wonder, "Where's this coming from?" Most things we struggle with are not on the surface level but much deeper.

It's why Paul himself said, "What I want to do I do not do, but what I hate I do." So, growth is a process of learning everything we need to learn and unlearning everything we need to unlearn too.

And, those deep things can all be changed.

Internalize this:

> **Search me, God, and know my heart; test me and know my anxious thoughts. See if there is any offensive way in me, and lead me in the way everlasting.**
>
> **Psalm 139:23**

Someone once suggested you pretend for a minute that you were working in the Empire State Building the day King Kong climbed it. Actually, that was your first day on the job there.

You don't really know anything since it's your first day. It's nearly lunch time, and you look out the window to see King Kong climbing up the building. You know, part of you might just be willing to believe that this could just possibly be normal.

Why? Because it's your first day. You don't know what's normal and what's not. You might call your boss, but you'd be slightly apologetic for calling since you might be bothering him about nothing. "Um, Sir... there's a 25 foot hairy ape climbing the building here. I'm not sure this is a concern of yours but just thought you should know... maybe."

"Oh, and, uh, I think he's got Faye from accounting with him. She definitely looks like she's not liking that. Especially with all those planes shooting and all. Again, I'm new here, don't mean to bother you."

Now you're thinking if you see a giant fire breathing lizard coming down the street to fight King Kong, you're taking the rest of the day off.

Know the first day on the job is kind of the way we are when we are young. We don't know what is and is not normal or right for sure. Commit to undoing the false we took in and learning the truth.

Ask God to reveal these things to you and bring them up to the surface of your mind where you can now discriminate the true from the false.

Recognize that you're in that process and invite God to search your heart and renew your mind. Don't settle for just surface change.

Uncover so much that's deep.

And grow!

Reading: Romans 7:7-25

"Growth is a process of learning and unlearning."

Day 85

The Most Famous Football Folly
and Avoiding the Most dangerous Folly of Life

The Bible's all about making U-turns.

It says we all start life in the wrong direction since we all have rejected God. We need to make a firm decision to change direction and follow Him.

We start with the desire to be in the wrong direction, to stay apart from knowing God. All we need is the turn around, the turn to receiving Christ into our lives.

Many people deny their sin and just stay in the wrong direction.

They may compare to others and figure they're okay, call "sin" a disease instead of a choice, say it is culturally relative, or something like that.

Some become religious or "good" instead of making a decision for God and away from sin.

So many ways to complicate things, to foul it up and stay in the wrong direction! And it's a shame, because all anyone really needs is to really choose God and really turn from their sin.

In fact, the most essential thing to accomplish in life is to get turned around and headed in the right direction – toward God, in a relationship with Him through Christ.

The right direction is everything.

Internalize this:

> **Repent, then, and turn to God, so that your sins may be wiped out, that times of refreshing may come from the Lord.**
>
> **Acts 3:19**

One for the record books.

What may just be one of the biggest blunders in National Football League history had to do with a player named Jim Marshall of the Minnesota Vikings. Marshall recovered a fumble and then ran the wrong way with the ball... for 66 yards. Instead of heading for the opponent's end zone, giving his team a touchdown, he headed for his own end zone.

His teammates on the sideline kept yelling to him, but he kept running the wrong way. He probably just thought they were cheering him on. He probably ran faster and thought, "Man, they must be really happy with me right now. I hear them cheering!"

He must have heard the crowd, too, but thought they were saying something like, "Way to go, Jim". Really they were saying, "Where are you going, Jim?" He went all the way the wrong way and scored two points, a safety, for the other team.

As he danced and celebrated in the end zone (all by himself), he finally figured it out. Suddenly, no more dancing. He had every good intention as he ran that wrong direction too. But it was the wrong way.

Some run their whole life like this Jim Marshall blunder, in the wrong direction, staying apart from Christ. We may also have every good intention as we do. We may be trying real hard to be good or religious. Just being good or religious is like running faster in the wrong direction.

Know good intentions are not enough. Make the U-turn we all need. Turn from your sin and follow God. If you have once made that U-turn but swayed from that new direction as a follower of Christ, get back on it.

Avoid the biggest life blunder of staying in the wrong direction.

Let times of refreshing come!

Reading: John 19:16-21 and 20:1-8

**"Being in the right direction changes
the outcome of everything you do."**

Day 86

Thrilled at the DMV
and Thrilled to be the Light of the World

What's it mean to be the light of the world?

The Bible is clear that's what we are to be, but how's that supposed to look? It's meant to be a combination of a few things. Among those things are our actions and our words.

Now, it is very important to see, you must have both, not just one or the other. If you have just the words but not the life to back it up, you are just a noisy clanging gong with those words. If you have just the life but not the words, people may want what you have but not know how to get it.

The key is that the Lord has entirely changed you through and through, that you are a new creature in Christ, that you are alive in Him doing all to His glory. Then you'll have the life and say the words too. It's like finding a treasure. You get it, are changed, and you want to tell everyone where it is so they can get it too.

It doesn't mean you need to be perfect. No one is. It means you need to be in the right direction toward God, in relationship with Him, wanting Him above all.

You'll still have plenty of faults. But your attitude toward them is what counts. Be honest about them and seek their removal

So, to the actions and words, add this attitude to your faults and you have what it takes to be the light of the world.

Internalize this:

> **You are the light of the world. A town built on a hill cannot be hidden… In the same way, let your light shine before others, that they may see your good deeds and glorify your Father in heaven.**

> **Matthew 5:14-16**

I was so excited… at the DMV. (Now, you don't hear this every day.)

But I was thrilled because, although I didn't order my plates special, they seemed, at first, to come out that way. It looked like my new license plate was a Bible verse. The verse? Acts 25:4.

Now the plate actual read ACT5254, but the "5" on the end of ACT could pass for an "S". So, there you had it. From any distance, ACTS 25:4. Close enough, I thought. I couldn't wait to get to my Bible to check out what this verse said. After all, this was now my verse.

I thought of the many great verses that exist in Acts such as Acts 4:12 which says, "Salvation is found in no one else, for there is no other name under heaven given to men by which we must be saved." Maybe it was like Acts 1:8. "But you will receive power when the Holy Spirit comes on you; and you will be my witnesses."

Perhaps, I thought, it was one like these. So I quickly looked up the verse in great anticipation. Was it one of those great verses? No. My verse read, "Festus answered, 'Paul is being held at Caesarea, and I myself am going there soon.'"

What?! Festus… my verse is a verse about Festus? Who is Festus? I don't know. No one does. Oh well.

But it's okay if our license plate doesn't proclaim the gospel. We have the opportunity with our life to tell other people about Christ. We have our words to tell them of Christ too.

Use your words, use your life and lead others to Christ. Be honest about your faults with the right attitude about them.

Know it's this combination that makes us a light.

Be that light!

Reading: Acts 1:1-8

**"We can be the light of the world
– faults and all."**

Day 87

A Scoreless Tie in Our Backyard and Coming Home to the Father's Arms

For many of us, we know that we need to make a decision to follow God. We just haven't quite done that yet.

You might say, it is on the agenda, the proverbial "to do" list. It just hasn't been checked off. You believe in God. But really choosing him? Still no. We figure that someday we will do something about it and really choose God. We are close to that item on our list a lot of the time. But, we just figure some other time would be better.

It could be a busy schedule or a friend who is closed off to God who kinda influences us. Maybe it's a fear we will have to give up something we just can't live without. Maybe it's a fear someone will laugh at us or think we are not worthy of following God.

Something always gets in the way of making that choice. It's like we are on a journey with some unexpected turns. We get lost on the way. We are trying to get home.

Whatever the reason, we end up putting it off. And, there remains in us that real deep need that says, "I need God". And we still are not "home".

We grow more and more weary as we let our life continue without the deep longing for God met. That tug of God on our hearts remains.

Getting home to God needs to be first on the "to do" list. It needs to be now.

Internalize this:

> **Even the sparrow has found a home, and the swallow a nest for herself, where she may have her young— a place near your altar, Lord Almighty, my King and my God.**

> **Psalm 84:3**

Another scoreless tie!

Where I grew up, we played baseball in a field next to my house. Now, looking back, I am a little puzzled by how we did things as kids.

First base was like a stick on the ground or something. Second base might have been a flat rock. But for some strange reason, third base was always this big old tree. What… were there no more sticks or rocks in the entire woods nearby?

You would get to first just fine. Then second. But come to third and then, splat. You're out cold. I hope there weren't any head-first slides into third but I bet there were.

Come to think of it, did anyone actually score a run in all those years? Was it nothing but scoreless ties? No one making it past that big old third base tree? Might have been!

Why we made third base a tree, I'll never know. But, that scenario actually plays out in our lives in many ways. For some, we know we need to be in the loving arms of our heavenly Father living for Him. But we've never made it… home.

We've made it to first, second, maybe third – we've thought about it a lot. We have almost made a decision for Him. But, that's it. We have put up some obstacle along the way. We still long for Him – still not in His arms.

It's time to come home.

God awaits. Put it off no longer. Remove that obstacles. Accept Him.

Know He is right there waiting for you. Don't stay on first, second, or third with good intentions, outside of His loving care.

Come all the way home!

Reading: Psalm 84

**"Coming to God is coming home…
and there's no place like home."**

Day 88

Reserved Parking a Mile Away
and Being a True Leader

Leadership.

There's lots of misconceptions about it.

And, with so many people "leading", you'd think the meaning of it would be clear. It's not, based on the results we see.

The Bible tells us what effective leadership really is. Jesus made it clear, "The great among you is the servant." Jesus said He did not come to be served but to serve and to give His life as a ransom for many. He washed His disciples' feet to demonstrate His servant-hood to them. He told them to do likewise.

Servant-hood is a commitment to the needs of others and meeting those needs by what we do and become. Using our skill and being committed to others in this way is one of life's greatest joys and God's call on our life.

This is why it is the servant we seek out in times of trouble. The servant knows our needs and can deal with them in the right way. This is leadership. So, saying the servant is the leader is not a cliché, it is the truth.

Being self-seeking is the opposite. It is a take from others. We don't seek that person out to lead.

So, the true servant is truly the leader making the biggest difference in the lives of others.

Internalize this:

> **Whoever wants to become great among you must be your servant, and whoever wants to be first must be your slave – just as the Son of Man did not come to be served, but to serve, and to give his life as a ransom for many.**
>
> **Matthew 20:26-28**

Is that sign in the right place?

I was out walking once and came across a hulking, big church. This church was huge, and it was surrounded by acres of parking lot. It was empty at that early hour, so I walked around the huge parking lot.

Way, way, way at the end of the lot was the sign that read: "Reserved for the Pastor". This spot was like a mile away from the church. It was hard to tell it was actually still in a part of the parking lot of the church. It was way out by the dumpster, too. You have to swat the birds and bugs away and pick up some blowing trash just to get out of your car.

Now I thought about that a great deal. I loved that sign being there. It seems that sign was a statement about the servant-hood of the pastor. That's what the sign meant. That's why it was at the end of the lot.

The Pastor was there to be last.
The Pastor was there to look out for others first.
The Pastor was clearly there to serve.

I saw another church's parking lot where there was also a "Reserved for the Pastor" sign. But this one was right by the entrance. He got the best spot. That sign seemed to say, "I'm first and most important. You go find your spot."

Know that we do the same things in our own lives. Sometimes we live as if the sign is in the back as a servant, sometimes as if it right by the entrance. And, all the while we want to lead.

Choose servant-hood. Know the needs of others and put yourself in a position to meet those needs.

Wash the feet of others. Know that's leadership.

Put your "sign" in the back.

Reading: Philippians 2:1-18

"The 'leader is a servant' is not just to be a cliché."

Day 89

Banana Slugs as a Team Name
and Living up to Our Names

What's in a name?

When it comes to the things God has to say about us – a great deal.

Often names mean things and represented qualities about you. Notice how Jesus changed Simon's name to Peter, which means rock. It was to show how mightily he would be used by God in the life of the early church.

Think about some of the names that have been given to you as well. You have been called the light of the world, child of God, temple of the Holy Spirit, beloved, holy, brothers and sisters, the redeemed. These are all things that are true of you as a faithful believer.

How significant to realize this!

We are to know we are forgiven, that He is our Father, that the Holy Spirit dwells in us, that we are to live holy lives, that we are united in Christ with other believers, that we are to be a light to all.

All just from our names. And we are to live up to those names just as Peter did and be a rock, a light, a great example.

What impact the names God has given can have if we take them to heart.

Internalize this:

> **But you are a chosen people,**
> **a royal priesthood,**
> **a holy nation,**
> **a people belonging to God.**
>
> **1 Peter 2:9**

I think it's finally happening.

Sports leagues are running out of names for their teams. The great names are already taken. There are just so many good animals like Tigers, Lions, and Bears. They are down to things like the Banana Slugs and Wet Sox. Yes, these are actual names of teams.

One team was even called the City Council. How do they intimidate other teams with names like that? "Those city council meetings can go really long!" Yes, there are no names left.

Some try to work names with adjectives like Mighty Ducks and Fighting Daisies but that doesn't work. I'm not at all concerned with the might of a duck. A daisy can't fight, nor, I suspect, would it want to.

But, one of my favorites is a minor league baseball team named the Tourists. How does that name work? Tourists are people who don't know what they're doing or where they're going. They are just trying to relax. They are not from around here.

What can they say to intimidate the other team? "We pack faster than you!" "We can see more sights in a day than you can!" "You should see us fold a map!" What logo can they use for their uniforms? A hotel? A GPS? Okay, let's go with luggage.

I saw a photo of the manager of the Tourists yelling at an umpire. Now you might think he's yelling at a bad call. I think he was just yelling because his name was Tourists, he couldn't motivate the team with that name, and he had luggage on his cap.

Your names are not like that at all. God has not run out of great names for you. Take them to heart and live your life in light of them.

Be the light of the world. Live as a child of God. Walk as part of a holy people.

For such you are.

Reading: 1 John 3:1-10

"You are a child of God. Live up to who you are."

Day 90

Scrambling for Foul Balls
and God's Great Providence

Trust, trust, TRUST God will take care of you!

He said he would. He wants you to know it and live it. So, He tells us it over and over. Just listen to these statements about trust in Scripture:

"He gives to His beloved even in their sleep."
"Lions go hungry but those who fear the Lord lack no good thing."
"[If you] know how to give good gifts to your children, how much more does your heavenly Father?"

Think of how differently we would go about life if we really know this to be the case.

We wouldn't envy. No need to.
We wouldn't covet. We would be thankful.
We wouldn't doubt. We would believe.
We would share, give and hope the best for other's too.

Things like worry, fear, complaining would also be out the window.

Trust is much better!

And, God's demanded it!

Internalize this:

> **The Lord will watch over your coming and going both now and forevermore.**

> **Psalm 121:8**

"I got it. I got it." I have always wanted to catch a ball hit into the stands at a baseball game. Now, I'm not picky. It could be a foul ball or home run ball. Either would be fine with me. Who wouldn't want that? That's exciting. There is only one obstacle to this, the 50,000 or so other fans who would also like to get a ball. Not easy.

To be honest with you, though, I'm not sure how some of these people even survive the balls hit into the stands. I mean, think about it. What other sport do they allow small objects moving at some 100 mph into crowds of people?

Out on the street they call that a shooting.

Sometimes people go through an awful lot to try to get a ball and never even end up with it. The ball comes and hits them first, knocks them out cold. Then the guy next to them just picks it up. He even stands up and is elated at his fortune. He is on camera. People cheer… for him.

No camera on the medical personnel taking care of the first guy or the ambulance taking him to the hospital... all with no ball. In the end, that hurt guy just stopped the ball for the guy who ended up with it. Oh that's not right!

There should be a rule out there in the stands. It would go like this, "If a ball is hit and, as a result, you're the one with a big mark on your head or tattoo that reads 'Spalding', you get the ball." And, all publicity and cheering must go to that hurt guy too… even if he won't hear any of it being unconscious and all.

That's why I was really glad when we were at a game one day and we got two balls. Yes two… the easy way. Someone who works at the stadium saw my two kids. Left for a while and came back with two balls for them. That was it. No welts. No wrestling anyone else in the stadium. They were ours.

Know this is the way God often provides. Put away wrestling with other people to get your way. Put away grumbling, envy, covetous and fear too. Put away everything that comes from a lack of trust. Be giving, caring and everything else God calls us to as a result of trust!

Know He watches over your coming and going both now and forevermore and gives to His beloved even in their sleep so you lack no good thing.

Trust!

Reading: Psalm 1

"Envying, coveting, or complaining and Trusting God are opposites."

Day 91

A Vacation in Paradise
and the Joy of Ministry

There is great joy in ministry.

In fact one of the things I like telling people, and it is almost always true, is that I often get more out of ministering then anyone I minister to. I trust, they are often greatly blessed, but still I'm more usually.

Most who minister would say the same.

That is just the nature of what we do in ministry… we get blessed and we bless. Ministry is powerful both for those we minister to and to us as we minister.

So for so many reasons, to be in ministry is the wisest thing we could be doing – to answer the call of what God has for our lives – to really be doing the things we have been created to do.

These things are wonderful. They bring joy. They are powerful. Not necessarily easy, simple, light, or noticeably fruitful all the time, but a blessing at a deeper level to everyone.

Ministry, of course, is just what the Bible tells us to do. Christ's final words in the Gospel of Matthew say it all. We are told to go. We are told He will be with us to direct and guide and keep us strong in Him as we do.

We are told of the great joy in ministry, too, for Jesus himself said, "It is better to give than to receive."

Internalize this:

> **Therefore go and make disciples of all nations, baptizing them in the name of the Father and of the Son and of the Holy Spirit, and teaching them to obey everything I have commanded you. And surely I am with you always, to the very end of the age.**
>
> **Matthew 28:19-20**

I have had a lot of good vacations like most people. But one place I really like to go is a couple of tropical islands just off the coast of Florida, Sanibel and Captiva. I particularly like going in the cold winter months. I love just getting off the plane and feeling that warm air in the middle of what was winter… up 'till then.

It felt like the place was having a big, warm winter party and loving it all and not telling any of us up North. But I was on to them.

And these islands were beautiful. Not a single traffic light. Large portions of land dedicated as wildlife preserves. Beautiful beaches… just about everything nice. I use to think that at least Christmas was still better everywhere else.

But then, ever see palm trees with Christmas lights? Love that too!

So, it was interesting for me when one day I was to speak in a church close to the islands. I figured I would go on vacation at the islands and in the middle, go speak. I just assumed that the highlight of that vacation would be the beaches, the palms, and the wildlife.

I was wrong. As good as all that was, it didn't compare to the powerful Sunday I had at the church in the middle of the vacation. That Sunday was clearly the highlight. In fact, to this day, I remember that Sunday and not anything of the rest of that vacation.

From that point on, I saw those islands and ministry a little bit differently. When I thought of the islands I thought how they couldn't hold a candle to the joy of true ministry in the Lord. This is not to take away anything from the islands. I still stand in awe of them. It's just that now I stand in even more awe of ministry than I ever did before.

Simply put, know that ministry, when you are in your calling, is better than a vacation in paradise. Don't miss out on the joy of ministering and what it will do… for you and others.

"Therefore, go."

Reading: Philippians 4:1-9

"Ministry in the Lord is better than a vacation in paradise."

Day 92

Forgetting a Dinner Reservation
and Remembering the Promises of God

Promises, promises!

I'm sure you have had some people in your life that have gone back on some promises they have made. You have had people lie to you and mislead you saying one thing and doing another.

But these are the promises or claims of sinful people not a holy and perfect God. The promises of a holy and perfect God always come to pass. He has never reneged on a promise and He never will.

Have you ever stopped to think about all the promises God has made to you and to every believer? There are a lot. Like:

He will never leave you. He will always perfect you.
He will guide you into His will. He has great plans for you.
He remembers your sin no more. He has heaven awaiting the faithful.

And, that's just a few. Sometimes these things He promises may seem impossible. Sarah thought that she could not have a child at her old age even though God said she would. She laughed at Him… then soon later, gave birth.

It's a game-changer when we really take His promises to heart, really believe they will be fulfilled and are being fulfilled. No wonder God says to always trust in His promises…

… they all come true.

Internalize this:

> **Every good and perfect gift is from above, coming down from the Father of the heavenly lights, who does not change like shifting shadows.**
>
> **James 1:17**

Even though I'm not that old, I still have my "senior" moments of forgetfulness. I hear more are on their way.

I can remember one time making a reservation for a restaurant. Then, I forgot I made that reservation. Worse though, I actually went out that day to the same restaurant and ate there. While seated, I saw a reserved sign on what was supposed to be MY table.

As we ate, I remember thinking how bizarre that someone would make a reservation and then never show. I was indignant with this rude, forgetful guy. And they watched his table so diligently! I soon realized who that rude guy was and why he "didn't" show.

I left hoping no one would catch on as I sheepishly got out – "reserved" sign still up. Table still empty. I felt like feigning disgust and saying something like, "The nerve of those people to make a reservation and not show." Hoping this would throw them off the track.

I forgot my "promise" to come. That's how we often do life and how we so frequently are to others. Sometimes, without even realizing it. We break promises. We may even get used to it in ourselves and others. Just accept this is the way things are. Sometimes we do it intentionally. Sometimes it's out of forgetfulness perhaps. Same for others.

But know this is never the case with God. He remembers every promise He has made to you. Know that all these promises will come to pass in the timing for them God has.

Know He will never leave you, always cares for you, answers every prayer, has pardoned all your sin, will give you eternity in heaven through Christ.

Remember all those promises and every other!

He will!

Reading: Genesis 18:1-15 and 21:1-6

"Remember God never forgets His promises."

Day 93

A Diet You Can Really Keep and Decision-making You Can Really Count On

"Today is the day of salvation."

So often young people will say things like… "You know, I will make a decision for the Lord when I am older" or "I'll start really living for God after I graduate" or something like that.

One problem is that in the meantime, they are going to go ahead and make all kinds of decisions that will impact the rest of their lives… all while they are not faithful to God.

We are likely to choose our career and our spouse both before we are thirty or so. We form significant patterns for relationships early on by our choices. Probably make some important education decisions. These are some of the biggest decisions we make, all when young. We want to make our decisions while we know God is guiding us as our Shepherd and we're following.

It's no wonder then the Bible says that "Today is the day of salvation". Now is the time to live faithfully with God. Now is the time to lay a foundation of wise decisions for your life.

This is true for every stage of life. We all have some decisions coming up. Waiting until those decisions are already come and gone before we choose to be faithful, may have great consequences.

The best choices are made when God is our Lord.

Internalize this:

> **Don't let anyone look down on you because you are young, but set an example for the believers in speech, in conduct, in love, in faith and in purity.**
>
> **1 Timothy 4:12**

There are definitely a few things in the way life is designed that I would consider reversing if I could.

For example, how about some of the foods that are good for you and not? Like wouldn't it be great if you could eat as much chocolate cake as you can but really make sure you lay off the carrots? That would be fun as a parent. "Kids, lay off the carrots. If you are going to snack, we have plenty of chocolate." "Yeah, Dad! You rock."

If I were a doctor I would love it too. I could say, "Sir, in your condition you had better start filling up on pizza and keep away from that oatmeal you keep having. It's killing you." Or, "Hey, you have put on some weight. You should cut down on all that exercise, take two doughnuts, make sure they're the chocolate kind with some sort of rich filling, and call me in the morning." "I love you, Doc."

There are some other things that might be fun to just reverse. How about the energy level of parents and their kids? Why is it that the parents who are responsible for taking care of the kids have no energy while the kids who need to accomplish nothing are bouncing off the walls? In fact you kind of know you are an adult when you go from hating to take a nap to dying for one at about 2:00 pm every day.

But one thing I also might reverse is how many big decisions we need to make early in life when we don't know as much, versus the ones we make later in life, when we know a little more. But, this can't be reversed either.

Know you will make big decisions early on in life, bigger than maybe any others you will need to make.

Be following God even at a young age. Make all those decisions you have coming up with God as your Lord.

Keep faithful to Him at every age too. There are always some important decisions to make.

Make all your decisions with God as Lord over the choice.

Reading: 1 Timothy 4:9-16

"The best decisions made are the ones made while God is your Lord."

Day 94

Cheerleaders at Your Job
and the Importance of Giving Support

Life is not a solo practice.

You're not meant to stand idly by while other people live their lives. You're not meant to just watch them struggle or see them enjoy their success in solitude.

No, you're meant to be someone who helps people through struggles and celebrates them in their successes. It has been said that shared sorrow is halved and shared joy is doubled.

Cain did not care about Abel to the point that he killed him. When asked by God where Abel was, Cain just replied, "Am I my brother's keeper?" Cain expected the answer to be "No." He thought it was a rhetorical question. But he was completely wrong.

The reality is "Yes." You are your brother's keeper – meant to help others, care for them and lead them on to all God has for them.

As a result, Cain lost a great opportunity to love others and leave a great impact. We seek to avoid his attitude to others. We say "Don't raise Cain" and everyone knows just what we mean.

Instead, the concerns of others should matter to us. In fact, we are even told by Scripture to count other's needs as more important than our own.

We are not meant to just play solitaire with life.

Internalize this:

> **Encourage the fainthearted, help the weak, be patient with everyone. Make sure that nobody pays back wrong for wrong, but always try to be kind to each other and to everyone else.**

> **1 Thessalonians 5:14-16**

"Go Team! Go! T-E-A-M. Go, go, go!"

We have all seen cheerleaders on the sidelines at a big football game. With every play, you can hear them screaming, the pom-poms are in the air, human pyramids are formed. They not only cheer, but they urge on the whole stadium to cheer, too. Before you know it, the crowd is yelling out things too, like DE-FENSE! DE-FENSE!

The players sense this excitement of the crowd and use it to step up their game. The home team has a decided advantage in football in part because of it and wins a disproportionate amount of the games… even though the field itself is exactly the same dimensions in any stadium.

So, why is cheerleading relegated to just sports? I think we need to have it at all our jobs and with everything we need to do. Imagine what work would be like with ten people yelling, "Go, go, go. Staple those papers, collate, collate!" How 'bout at school? "Take those notes! Take them, take them. Sharpen that pencil! Way to use that scrap paper! Learn, learn. Go… Jim!!" It would be great in relationships, "Love that wife. Value her, value her, L-O-V-E H-E-R!"

Add some flips and pyramids and you really have it going. I would also like one of those mascot guys hanging around me too, giant head and all. A marching band playing would be a nice touch. You may want to get office approval for these things first.

Cheering for others seems to work with just about everything. Now I mean real cheering. The kind of cheering that really looks out for others, challenges others, celebrates others victories, carries burdens, and also corrects others at times too.

Most jobs and most roles in life have far too little cheering for others going on. Be a cheerleader in the lives of others because it will always change them and make them better.

Don't play solitaire when it comes to life. Be there for others in every way. Cut sorrows in half. Double joys.

Be your 'brother's keeper'.

Reading: Genesis 4:1-12

"Life is not meant to be a game of solitaire."

Day 95

Standing Up for a Turkey
and a Lesson On Being Great

Ever blown it?

When you make a mistake, it's really easy to get very down. And the more you dwell on it, the worse it gets. You're actually even more likely to make a mistake with your next decision or action if you can't get over it.

When you make a mistake you've got to find a way to put it behind you. It's no wonder the name Satan means "accuser". He wants those errors right in front of you, dogging you for years. Mistakes gain undue influence when they're allowed to linger.

One helpful thing is to realize that every great person has made plenty of mistakes. The Bible makes sure we know just how mistake-ridden the heroes of the faith were. In fact, few escaped great error. There was Jacob with his deception, David with his adultery, and Peter with his denials, just to name a few.

They went on to be a patriarch, a man after God's own heart, and a rock of the early church. The Bible shows us these things so we know just what to do when we make our own mistakes.

We are to get right back in the way of faithfulness and not let mistakes influence what is coming next. It's not that we don't care about mistakes or seek to learn from them. We do! But we also understand the grace of God and need to move on in order to succeed.

We are to be like Jacob, David, and Peter!

Internalize this:

> **Though a righteous man falls seven times, he rises again, but the wicked are brought down by calamity.**
>
> **Proverbs 24:16**

Great statesman. A founding father of our nation. The whole kite and key experiment.

But while that's what we remember Ben Franklin for, he wasn't always so stellar. Here is an example. Strange but true, Ben Franklin did not like the eagle being the nation's symbol. In 1784 in a letter to his daughter, Franklin criticized the eagle saying it was "generally poor and often very lousy."

He concluded, "I wish the Bald Eagle had not been chosen." In the same letter he noted how the turkey would have been better. He said, "The turkey is in comparison a much more respectable bird."

Imagine if Franklin had chosen to really argue for the turkey. What would that have looked like? Can't you just see him on the floor of Congress? "Come on, my fellow Americans, with the turkey's red wattle hanging down from its chin and its 'gobble, gobble' sound, (imagine him very animated and gesturing with these words) how could we not go with the turkey as our national symbol?"

Nothing but blank stares and dropped jaws from everyone else in Congress. Finally, perhaps, someone tries to reach a compromise here and just put an end to Ben's blunder. "Ben, how 'bout we go with the eagle and someday celebrate Thanksgiving as a national holiday and we'll all have turkey?" Problem solved.

Remember, even the greats and everyone we know have their moments, their lapses in judgment, their foolishness.

I'm sure Franklin didn't let it linger on. He went on to many successful things. He was perhaps the greatest American Founding Father who never became President. A full 20,000 people attended his funeral. He's on money!

Determine that mistakes will never keep you from moving on to all you're called to do, all the wonderful things God has in store for you. Rise again if you fall!

That's what the greats do.

Remember the turkey.

Reading: Matthew 26:69-75 and Acts 2:14-21

"Every great one has also played the fool."

Day 96

Being Extra Minute Guy
and Having a Great Prayer Life

One thing to cherish is a great prayer life.

There are many reasons for that. One is that prayer is simply very effective. We are told that prayer is always effective. God always hears our prayers and it always affects the outcome in some way. If a business found something that always worked, they would always do it. That's a good policy we can apply to prayer.

Sometimes we don't see how it has affected the outcome because it's not as we expect. The answer comes much later or God answers in a much better way than we may think. The only way we should want it anyway.

It has been said, "God does not stoop to answer prayer in our way. He answers in His way."

Another significant reason to cherish a great prayer life is due to how much it changes us and who we are. The process of speaking to God is dramatic to shape our outlook, our focus, our interpretation of events.

We go through life differently when we go through life in prayer.

We are also told that prayer is always effective in blessing the Lord. In fact, the Bible says that the prayers of believers are like incense rising up before God as a soothing aroma to Him.

And, a balanced prayer life has more than just requests. It has praise, thanksgiving, and confession, too. All powerful to life!

How precious is a great prayer life!

Internalize this:

> **The prayer of a righteous person is powerful and effective.**
>
> **James 5:16**

Cell phones are like relationship barometers.

Let me explain. With the cell phone, people might call at very odd times. You get calls at 6:55 am… unlimited minutes before 7:00 am. You get calls 9:01 each night, same reason.

One guy called me to chat just because he had extra minutes that month. Now, how can you start a conversion like that and expect the other person to want to actually talk to you?

I don't want to be the extra minute guy you call. I want to be the overage guy. You know, the one whom you call when it's gonna cost you more than your plan. Now, that would be a conversation starter. "Hello. I'm totally out of minutes but you're worth it!"

You can define entire relationships based on when the call is being made. Overage… we are going places. Extra minutes… not so much.

With the dropped call, you can also tell how important the conversation is by how quickly someone tries to get the call back. There is always that call that gets dropped and neither try to call back. A month later, the two see each other: "Did we drop a call a month back?" "I guess we did."

When and where we call on God may indicate something about our relationship with Him, too. Is it really that frequent, balanced prayer life God calls us to? Or is it sporadic, maybe only when we are in distress? Is it just requests, never praise, thanksgiving or confession?

Make your prayer life dynamic. Make it a reflection of an excellent walk with God.

Know this is the prayer life God desires. Know prayer always works, always changes you, and is a soothing aroma to God.

Pray!

Reading: 1 Kings 17:17-24 and James 5:13-18

**"You go through life differently when
you go through life in prayer."**

Day 97

The Most Dangerous Tool in the Shed and the Dangerous Nature of Sin

Our natural inclination is to sin!

That's really important to know. What that means is that if we are going to overcome sin in our lives, it will take an effort. Sin doesn't just go away. It must be willfully and emphatically removed.

We have to treat sin like that guest who has stayed over way too long. We need to show it the door.

With an unwanted guest, you still have to be kinda polite in how you ask them to leave. With sin, you don't have to be. You can just be firm and definitively remove it from your life.

We find all kinds of ways to sort of keep sin around, too. We can blame others for it being around. We can justify our actions to keep it around. Compromise a bit.

There's a phrase that goes, "You don't negotiate with terrorists." In a way, sin is a form of terrorism. It takes us hostage to things that hurt us. Negotiating in any of these ways, isn't the way to go.

Instead, the Bible tells us to "die to sin".

It would be nice if our natural inclination were to holiness.

It's not.

Internalize this:

We died to sin; how can we live in it any longer?

Romans 6:2

It's funny the things we have phobias over.

I have a fear of heights. When I am in high places, I often stay away from the edges – even if there's a railing. They make the railings too short! I somehow think that I may just involuntarily leap over the railing. I need railings that go over my head. Well, I guess that would be a cage. Yes, then, a cage is what I need when I am high up.

People ask, "If you are afraid of heights, why aren't you afraid of flying?" That's simple. I would fear it if I were on the wing of the plane. As it is, I am inside eating peanuts. Peanuts are medicinal. You can't fear anything while eating peanuts! It's why so many squirrels get hit by cars. They're eating nuts and fearing nothing.

I felt a little vindicated about my fear of heights when I found out what tool in the shed is the most dangerous. It's the ladder!

There are lots of other fears out there. Fear of snakes is a big one. One thing that helps me with that is the numbers. Did you know only about one person per year dies of snakebite in the entire U.S.? There's a phobia of long words too. It's called, hippopotomonstrosesquipedaliophobia. Yea – whoever named that was obviously messing with those who actually have the fear.

One thing is always true of things we have phobias about though – we keep a distance from the object, whether it is heights, snakes, big words, or anything else. We have that kind of natural reaction to them thinking they may harm us.

Know that we don't have that same natural reaction to stay far from sin even though it produces the greatest harm to our lives. Make the clear and certain effort that needs to be made to distance yourself from sin. Show it the door. Die to sin and live to God. Don't blame, justify, or compromise about it all instead.

Treat sin as the harmful 'terrorist' it really is.

Don't negotiate.

Reading: 1 Corinthians 10:1-13

"Handle sin and terrorism the same way. Don't negotiate!"

Day 98

Empty Seats at the Super Bowl and the Greatness of Knowing God

Many just don't realize how great it is to know God and follow Him.

Maybe they think it's just a bunch of rules and regulations. Very empty. To them it's a mere religion of sorts, not actually knowing God.

For some they just see it as restrictive. God takes away all the fun. So, they don't follow Him. Empty again.

Many think that it is just their family tradition and keeping up with what you do as a family. Maybe a cultural thing too. This is not fellowship with God either.

Instead of any of these things, knowing God is the most dynamic and greatest thing we could ever experience. It is being reunited with our loving Creator – the very purpose of our life.

Following Him is our greatest need. The thing we were made to be doing. How great when we actually are in a relationship with God.

So great He says give up all and follow Him.

So great He says to make the decision for Him and never look back.

So great He says everything else is like rubbish compared to knowing Him.

Internalize this:

> **I consider everything a loss compared to the surpassing greatness of knowing Christ Jesus my Lord, for whose sake I have lost all things. I consider them rubbish that I may gain Christ.**

> **Philippians 3:7**

Did you know that the first Super Bowl had 38,000 empty seats? That's right. They couldn't sell this thing out or even close to it. Cameramen tried not to show the empty sections all game.

I wonder what that would be like, trying to sell Super Bowl tickets and people turning you down. "What? Super what? Are you selling big bowls? No thanks. I've got lots of them at home... and they're plenty super." The tickets then only cost $6, $10, and $12. Wow. For $15 I wonder if they would let you sit with the teams. For $20 I'll bet you could play.

What would it have been like if you bought too many tickets for that Super Bowl and tried to sell your extra? "Please, I overbought... how about $2 for the remaining five I have?" People who have paid a few thousand for a ticket are cringing about now.

Imagine that, you could put your coat in the seat next to you and your feet up on the seat in front of you... at the Super Bowl. Ushers are like, "It doesn't matter, sit wherever you want."

There are not empty seats at the Super Bowl now. Except maybe that one guy or two for whom everything always goes wrong. They say, "I had a ticket but..." You can fill in the blank. Short of that, the stadium is full.

It can be that way when we talk about God to others. They just figure this is not something worth it. They refuse it as if it is something undesirable. They pass up a great thing, life in Christ, like leaving an empty seat at the Super Bowl.

There shouldn't be empty seats at the Super Bowl. And there should not be anyone refusing to know God and follow Him with all they are either. Know following God is not the way many think of it. Know it's not empty rules, taking all the fun out of life, or mere tradition.

Consider everything to be rubbish compared to the surpassing greatness of knowing Christ.

Give up all and follow Him.

Get your seat!

Reading: 2 Corinthians 5:17-6:2

"Nothing compares to the surpassing greatness of knowing Christ Jesus."

Day 99

"I've Seen that Movie Twenty Times" and How to Know the Bible Well

Learning the Bible well is a lot like everything else. It comes with time and effort. It comes with repetition.

This may be what God is after in passages like this, "Let the word of Christ dwell in you richly."

Joshua said he meditates on the Word day and night. Repetition! Time! Effort!

Jesus modeled knowing the Bible by memory. He rebuked the devil with passages that He knew from the top of His head.

Sure, a seminary degree would be nice. How 'bout a doctorate in theology? Yes, very good. Most people will not go to Seminary or get their doctorate though.

For most people, learning the Bible will come by repetition, time, and effort at their church and home.

What a goal!

Internalize this:

> **For the word of God is living and active. Sharper than any double-edged sword, it penetrates even to dividing soul and spirit, joints and marrow; it judges the thoughts and attitudes of the heart.**

> **Hebrews 4:12**

Is there a movie you like to watch over and over?

I have a few of those. I am surprised to find that I'm not alone. In fact, so many people have a number of movies they have watched more than five times, some more than ten or twenty.

It's interesting what starts to happen when you watch a movie that often. You notice things no one else has noticed. You see many things you miss the first time around. You also start internalizing lines and saying them as part of your conversations.

Now it really gets good when two people who both have the same movie they have watched twenty times get together. Ever hear them talk? They converse back and forth with the lines of the movie.

Sometimes they cover entire scenes together going back and forth with the lines they have memorized. Everyone around wonders what is going on… haven't seen the movie.

You can also tell a lot about a person by which movie they have watched over and over. There are the "Gone with the Wind" people and "Weekend at Bernie's Two" people. Enough said.

Did you know that it could be just that way with God's Word? The average reader will read about 3 ½ chapters of the Bible in about 15 minutes. At that pace, they would read the Bible through in a year if they simply gave that 15 minutes every day.

Now that means over a period of say ten years, the daily reader would have read through the Bible ten times. Now, you see it starts getting like those movies we watch over and over. We know what is in the Bible and not. We start having the verses memorized. We are reciting them over and over… they are a big part of our life. We even converse differently with others who know the Word too.

All just from that short time every day.

Make going through the Bible often your goal. Know the Word is sharp as a two-edged sword. Put in the repetition over time that leads to learning so much.

Let the Word richly dwell in you. Meditate on it day and night.

And, you don't even need popcorn to do it.

Reading: Revelation 22:13-21

"The best thing to have in your memory is the Bible."

Day 100

Being a Bapticostedistepiscaterian and Walking in Unity with Other Believers

Majoring on the minors.

Don't do it! It's one of the reasons believers don't walk in unity as they could. Only a few things are major. We know what they are - salvation in Christ alone, the one who is fully God and man who died on the cross for our sins. We must accept Him into our lives to go to heaven. The Bible is wholly true in all it affirms. These are majors.

We make so many other things major though. Whether it be our view of church government, styles of worship, our End Times theology, and other comparatively small things like that. Hey, it's true. The minors are important. But they are not major. And when we treat them as major, they are harmful to the unity of Christ and our witness to the world. This is unacceptable.

It's the cause of so much unfortunate denominationalism. Reality is, what unites the true body of believers is far greater than the differences between us. This should show! This must show!

We really are one body, called to unity. It's this unity that will reach the world even more than all our programs and strategies. No wonder we are called to being as one.

Unity shows what's really major!

Christ.

Internalize this:

> **May [believers] be brought to complete unity. Then the world will know that you sent me and have loved them even as you have loved me.**
>
> **John 17:22-23**

Do you want to know my denomination? I'll tell you. I'm a Bapticostedistepiscaterian.

That's right. Try that word in spell check… it's not coming up. It's a mix of many denominations. Why? I have benefited so greatly from people from every denomination deeply over the years. Here's a few ways:

The person who lead me to Christ: Pentecostal
The church I attended as a new believer establishing me: Assemblies of God
My campus movement in college: Interdenominational
Our campus ministry director: Evangelical Free
A helpful church I attended in college: Christian and Missionary Alliance
Another helpful church I attended in college: American Baptist
My seminary for my Master's: Interdenominational, largely Reformed
My seminary for my Doctorate: Interdenominational, largely Southern Baptist
The denomination I first served as pastor: Assemblies of God
The school of my children: Interdenominational, largely Baptist
Churches I have served as head pastor: Presbyterian

Is it any wonder then that I am a Bapticostedistepiscaterian and wouldn't have it any other way?

Truth is, I bet you could say the same when you look back on your life. You could spot people and churches from across the spectrum who have greatly enriched your life. Maybe this is true and you don't even know it!

Know why this is - we are one body and God is working through us just like that. So, don't major on the minors. Leave out denominationalism and see what great things will come to you and what great things you will contribute by being open to the whole body of Christ.

Know how critical unity is and be sure you are walking in it. Know minors are minors. Keep only the major things major.

Know unity shows Christ to the world.

Reading: John 17:15-26

"Be a Bapticostedistepiscaterian."

Day 101

One Great Ski Trip
and A Message Worth Telling

You made it to the end! Congratulations. Most people don't finish what they start. You did. Well done. (Unless of course you just flipped to this one. Hey! Go back to the others!)

It is very important to finish a lot of the things we start in life. But the most important thing we finish that we have started is our walk with the Lord. We want to be someone who finishes well. We want it to be where we can say that we've been faithful to Him to the end. God is to be praised, loved, sought, enjoyed, and glorified by our lives to that last breath.

Affirming this of his own life, Paul said these very moving and significant words, "I have fought the good fight, I have finished the race, I have kept the faith." This is meant to be our testimony too! God promises that He will make this come to pass for all of us who choose to make it the end. "He will also keep you firm to the end, so that you will be blameless on the day of our Lord Jesus Christ." And we know, firm to the end is what God truly wants. The Bible says, "We want each of you to show this same diligence to the very end."

So, fight the good fight enduring to the end with a life of faith growing deeper every day. Finish well. Now, let me close these 101 Days just by telling you how I began what I intend to finish. The following is my personal testimony of coming to Christ.

Internalize this:

> **I have fought the good fight, I have finished the race,
> I have kept the faith.**
>
> **2 Timothy 4:7**

A message worth telling.

The greatest decision in my life came when I was nineteen years old. Up to this time, I knew that whatever I was supposed to be living for, I didn't have. I had tried many things like being good and religious, having friends, making money, but knew none of those things was what I was meant to live for. I was empty.

As I went off to college for my first year at college, I determined to find out what I was supposed to live for. The quote I put with my high school yearbook senior picture expressed my desire to find out, "There will be an answer, let it be." Despite trying many things when I first got to college, I was still empty.

Then, on the winter break of that freshmen year, my cousin and I spoke. I knew that he had recently made a decision for God, but I didn't know much about what this meant. He explained that every person has a great void when they don't know God personally. We were meant to have a personal relationship with God through Jesus Christ. Jesus, fully God and fully man, died for our sins so that we can come to know God personally and be forgiven.

Without a relationship to God through Christ, we will be missing the greatest thing for our life – no matter how many other things we try. The next day, on my way to a ski trip, I realized I had been keeping God out of my life and that this was wrong. I opened the door of my heart and received Christ.

Right then, in a small ski lodge, Christ came into my life. I began the relationship with God I was always meant to have. I had new life in Christ being restored to my very purpose. I had always had a belief there was a God but never had a relationship with Him. I knew with this new relationship, I was forgiven before God for my sin and would spend eternity with Him in heaven.

I would seek to love God and others more and grow in my relationship with Christ over the days and years ahead. I would realize in an ever greater way God's endless love for me in Christ. The joy of knowing and following Him would become deeper and deeper. I knew He would always be there even in the midst of great trials. I realized this was the greatest decision, not only that I made, but that anyone could make.

Reading: The whole Bible!

"The most important decision anyone could ever make is the decision to know the Lord."

Epilogue

One day, when I was coaching a baseball team, I divided the team in half so we could scrimmage each other. Half our team versus the other half. I wanted to get them all in the game to see how each does and give each an opportunity to get better.

It seemed to work until I saw one player at the end of the scrimmage looking very sullen. I was like, "What's the problem?" To which he carefully but forcefully pointed out that I had overlooked him and him only. He, and only he, did not actually get in the game on either team.

I had a lot going on coaching both teams. I had a tough enough time coaching one team but two at once? Well, in the chaos, I forgot him and it hurt. Being overlooked always does.

Well, here's the thing. Someone once said that when we neglect to have our devotional time on any given day, it's like we overlooked God in a meeting we were meant to have with Him. Hmmm, that's not good.

Let's not overlook Him and have a daily devotional life.

You know, as a kid, I always wondered why those auto parts stores or home improvement places might be named something like "1001 Auto Parts" or "1001 Tools". I thought "What is their deal? Why don't they just round down to 1000 if they have 1001 parts or tools? Just forget that other one. Don't bother mentioning it!"

Well, of course, they meant that the first 1000 was just the beginning. It goes on from there. So, yes, these 101 days are also meant to be just a beginning of much more, of a daily devotional life your whole life.

Make that happen.

"Come close to God and he will come close to you." (James 4:8)

About the Author

Dr. Doug LaPointe has been in pastoral ministry for over twenty years and has also served as a school teacher, baseball coach, professor, golf instructor, and fried chicken cook (but it was very good chicken!).

He is currently the pastor of Cold Spring Church of Bristol, Tennessee, where he lives with his family (and his kids always do everything he tells them).

He is a graduate of Rutgers University (BA), Gordon-Conwell Theological Seminary (M Div), and Southern Evangelical Seminary (D Min). (Okay, that's enough schooling for now.)

Doug is also the author of *The Top 50 Questions Ever Asked about Christianity* which provides *"Life Changing Answers for the Devoted and the Doubtful"*. (Available on Amazon. But then again, what is not available on Amazon?)

Contact Doug with your comments or questions at: pastordouglapointe@gmail.com or visit him at Cold Spring. Visit online at coldspringchurch.org or on Facebook at Cold Spring Church. (It may even be church potluck day when you come… in which case, see Day 77.)

Notes, Commitments, and Prayers: